50 Principles For Becoming An Extraordinary Sales Person and Achieving More Success

MIKE DRIGGERS

Copyright © 2017 IME publishing group

ALL RIGHTS RESERVED no part of this book or its associated ancillary materials may be reproduced or transmitted in any form or by any means, electronic or mechanical, including photocopying, recording, or by any information of storage or retrieval system without the permission from the publisher.

PUBLISHED BY IME Publishing Group

DISCLAIMER AND/OR LEGAL NOTICES
While all attempts have been made to verify the information provided in this book and its ancillary materials, neither the author or the publisher assume any responsibility for errors, inaccuracies or omissions and is not responsible for any financial loss by consumer in any manner. Any slights of people or organizations are unintentional. If advice concerning legal, financial, accounting or related matters is needed, the service of a qualified professional should be sought. This book and its associated axillary materials, including verbal and written training, is not intended for use as a source of legal, financial or accounting advice. You should be aware of the various laws governing business transactions or other business practices in your particular geographical location.

EARNINGS AND INCOME DISCLAIMER
With respect to the reliability, accuracy, timeliness, usefulness, adequacy, completeness, and/or suitability of information provided in the book, Mike Driggers and IME Publishing Group its Partners Associates Affiliates Consultants and/or presenters make no warranties guarantees representations or claims of any kind. Readers results will vary depending on a number of factors. Any and all claims or representations as to income earnings are not to be considered and average earnings. Testimonials are not representative. This book and all products and services are for education and informational purposes only. Use caution and see the advice of qualified professionals. Check with your accountant, attorney or professional adviser before acting on this or any information. You agreed that Mike Driggers and IME Publishing Group is not responsible for the success or failure of your personal, business, health or financial decisions relating to any information presented by Mike Driggers and IME Publishing Group or Company products/services. Earnings potentials is entirely dependent on the efforts, skills and application of the individual person.

Any examples, stories, references, or case studies are for illustrative purposes only and should not be interpreted as testimonies and/or examples of what reader and/or consumers are generally expected from the information. No representation in any part of this information, materials and/or seminar trainings are guarantees or promises for actual performance. Any statements, strategies, concepts, techniques, exercises and ideas in the information materials and/or seminar training offered are simply opinion or experience, and thus should not be misinterpreted as promises, typical results or guarantees (expressed or implied). The author and the publisher (Mike Driggers, IME Publishing Group (IME) or any IME Representatives) Shall in no way, under any circumstances be held liable to any party (or third-party) for any direct, indirect, punitive, special, incidental or other consequential damages arising directly or indirectly from any use of books, materials and or seminar trainings, which is provided "as is," and without warranties

Mike Driggers / IME Publishing Group
www.SuccessWithMikeDriggers.com
www.IMEPublishingGroup.com

IME Publishing Group/ Mike Driggers —1st ed.
ISBN: - 978-0-9973034-6-9

PRINTED IN THE UNITED STATES OF AMERICA

WHAT OTHERS ARE SAYING ABOUT MIKE DRIGGERS AND HIS STRATEGIES

Recommend To All Leaders – Great Insights!
— **Daniel Eugene** "Rudy" Ruettiger, Played football for University of Notre Dame and In 1993, TRISTAR Productions immortalized his life story with the blockbuster film, "RUDY"

Mike Driggers principles offer a fresh and timely perspective that will ignite your soul and put fuel on your internal fire to go out and be the best you can be in your personal and professional life.
— **Jill Lublin**, CEO, PublicityCrashCourse.com, International Speaker & 4x Best selling Author

Whether you're a seasoned business leader, a recent graduate just starting your career or an entrepreneur, Mike Driggers principles and approach apply across all Industries and disciplines. Mike's attitude is inspiring and he is an outstanding mentor. — **Jonathan Atkinson**, Criminal Investigator Santa Clara County District Attorney's Office

Mike's ideologies to achieving everything you ever wanted in business and in Life gives you a step-by-step blueprint that will make you strive harder and push further than you ever have. — **Sonia Hinojo**, Air Liquid Sales and Marketing Manager

Mike's practical ways to becoming a high achiever in business and in your personal life through his simple to use principles are a must-have and I highly recommend you learn them now. — **Greg Kite**, Former NBA Player for the Boston Celtics & Executive Field Chairman for Hegemon Group International

GREAT meeting today--as usual, terrific atmosphere for connecting, and a great tactics and strategy exercise led by Mike. — **David Hirata**, Theatrical Modern Magician

I really appreciate the high quality of biz coaching my group has from Mike Driggers! — **Ellen Vaughn Simonin**, Physical Therapist and Acupuncturist

The ideas presented by Mike Driggers offer an inspiration and exciting perspective that will change the course of how you succeed in business or life. — **Steve Jones**, 10 years Law Enforcement

Whether you're an executive at a fortune 500 company or an entrepreneur Mike Driggers solutions go far beyond traditional business practices. Any organization can put this to immediate use and achieve amazing results. — **Steve Aust,** Former NBA Player for the Los Angeles Lakers, Chairman Co-Founder of Agora Advantage

Mike Driggers strategies are remarkable and insightful. He provides an easy-to-understand blueprint that makes you want to jump ahead and implement his process immediately. — **Belza López**, Housing Specialist for the City of Napa

Mike Driggers Concepts will become an invaluable tool in business and life for those who are on a pursuit of Excellence and Success. — **Gabriela Aguilera**, Orthodontic Treatment Coordinator

INSTANT AUTHORITY

Special **FREE** Bonus Gift For **YOU!**

To help you stand out from the crowd **FREE BONUS RESOURCES** for you at;
www.InstantAuthorityNow.com

FREE $997 VALUE

Get your 3 FREE in-depth training videos sharing how you gain trust from prospective customers. This trust will lead to establishing you as an authority, increase web traffic, boost business sales and attract more referrals. You will also learn how to earn the respect in your industry which can lead to more lucrative partnerships.

www.InstantAuthorityNow.com

Nothing In SALES Starts Until YOU Start

"Share This Book"

Retail 24.95
Special Quantity Discounts

5-20 Books	21.95
21-99 books	18.95
100-499 books	15.95
500-999 books	10.95
1,000 + books	8.95

To Order Go To www.BookMikeToday.com

THE IDEAL PROFESSIONAL SPEAKER FOR YOUR NEXT EVENT!

Any organization that wants to develop and grow their business to become "extraordinary" needs to hire Mike for a keynote and /or workshop training!

TO CONTACT OR BOOK MIKE TO SPEAK:

IME Publishing Group

(866) 7BOOKME

(866) 726-6563

www.BookMikeToday.com

Info@SuccessWithMikeDriggers.com

DEDICATION

*Many thanks and praises to GOD Almighty
who has guided me on the path that he has chosen for me.
This book is dedicated to my son Alex who is my driving spirit and
my greatest accomplishment in life.*

*My thanks go to my Mother and Father, who have always believed in
me and have encouraged me to reach for the stars.*

*A special thanks goes out to my sweetheart, Gaby Aguilera, who has
played a tremendous part in helping make this book a reality.
Also, greatthanks to James Malinchak who helped with the finer
details of the concepts. And special thanks to Ed Melliza photography.*

*Special thanks to all the great mentors, coaches and business partners
whose teachings have had a profound impact on my personal and
business life.*

CONTENTS

A Message To You xv
Introduction xix
Principle 1 Know Your Selling Principles 1
Principle 2 Be a Problem Solver 3
Principle 3 Customers Buy Because of Their Own Reasons 5
Principle 4 Customers buy what your product does, not the product itself 7
Principle 5 Sell with Honesty and Integrity 9
Principle 6 Be Positive Thinker 11
Principle 7 Don't Be Afraid of Rejection 13
Principle 8 Give Importance to the Customer 15
Principle 9 Develop a Prospecting Attitude 17
Principle 10 Learn How to Find Out Your Finest Lead Sources. 19
Principle 11 Know Exactly What a Prospect Is? 23
Principle 12 Learn How to Use Elevator Statements 25
Principle 13 Learn How to Use General Benefit Statements 27
Principle 14 Learn How to Do Pipeline Planning 29
Principle 15 Learn How to Do Pipeline Management 31
Principle 16 Demonstrate Your Intent and Desire to Help 33
Principle 17 Learn How to Overcome Call Reluctance 35
Principle 18 Learn How to Make a Positive First Impression 39
Principle 19 Always be a 'Curious' Questioner 41
Principle 20 Learn to Listen Up 43
Principle 21 Learn the P.O.G.O. Formula 45
Principle 22 Learn to Ask Questions Effectively to Uncover the Need 49
Principle 23 Learn How to Uncover the Need: The Prospect ... 51

Principle 24 Learn How to Make Use of Status Quo Questions 53

Principle 25 Learn to Read Non-verbal Cues from Your Prospect 55

Principle 26 Avoid Overwhelming the Prospect with Too Much Information..59

Principle 27 Know the Advantages of Presenting Your Product's Benefits Clearly 61

Principle 28 Bridge the Feature, Function, and Benefit to Your Prospect 63

Principle 29 Learn to Lead with Need 65

Principle 30 Learn How to Paint Word Pictures 67

Principle 31 Learn to Urge Your Prospect Emotionally to Take Action Today...69

Principle 32 Mind Your Body Language, Create a Good Impression...71

Principle 33 Learn How to Tap Into Your Prospect or Customer's Emotions 73

Principle 34 Maintain Eye Contact the Correct Way with Your Prospect 75

Principle 35 Learn How to Develop a 'Closing' Attitude 77

Principle 36 Learn to Make Use of Trial Closes 79

Principle 37 Learn the Three Tested and Reliable 'Asking for the Order' Closes 81

Principle 38 Learn the 4 Refined 'Persuade the Prospect to Agree and Buy' Closes 83

Principle 39 Learn to Try More Than Five Times to Ask For the Order 87

Principle 40 Always Maintain a Relationship with the Customer after the Sale 89

Principle 41 Learn to Ask for Referrals..91

Principle 42 Develop Voice Inflection and Voice Modulation....93

Principle 43 Learn to Love Questions and Objections 95

Principle 44 Learn The Right Time to Handle Objections and Questions Effectively 97

Principle 45 Learn How to Manage Objections 99

Principle 46 Do Value Added Selling 103

Principle 47 Learn to Upsell Every Time 105

Principle 48 Learn the Proper Telephone Skills 107

Principle 49 Learn to Use the Voicemail as a Tool 111

Principle 50 Learn to Use Email Effectively 115

One Last Message 117

Author Bio 121

NOTHING IN SALES STARTS UNTIL YOU START

A MESSAGE TO YOU!

Hi, I'm Mike Driggers, and I wanted to congratulate you on the wise decision to continue your education and the investment you just made in yourself..

I'm extremely proud of your decision to invest in you because you have literally done what most people will not do and I believe that this is the biggest reasons why people fail to achieve the results that they desire in their personal and professional lives.

Most people do not invest time or money into any type of continued education once they have finished schooling in order to learn new strategies that can create successful results. What's funny is that these are the same people that sit around complaining and blame society for their lack of success and it is never them. I am sure you are familiar with what I'm talking about. We all have either met or know someone who has this disease called excusitis. They use the "if it wasn't for" saying.

If it wasn't for the economy, president, location, my boss, I would have...

These are the type of people that always place blame on others issues. They would rather spend the time and focus on why it can't be done than making a decision to take action and focus on why they can and what they need to do to make it happen.

However, this is why you will stand out from the rest. You are different because you have decided to take action by continuing your education and investing in yourself. Because of this I have a incredible amount of respect for you.

One my favorite quotes that illustrates my point is

> *"I am not a product of my circumstances.*
> *I am a product of my decisions."* — Stephen Covey.

It is the mindset that makes a difference in your outcome. Every action has a reaction and the decision you make whether positive or negative determines the outcome. Making the decision to investment in yourself always has the highest returns. In all the courses and books I have spent money on I have never looked at it as spent money, I looked at it as I have invested in me just like you have with investing in you with this book.

I look at your decision as you want to be better and you have invested in yourself to do so. I believe your success will be in direct proportion to your continued personal development. I am in celebration for your decision not because you bought my book but because you are continuing to develop YOU.

Why did I put these principles together in a book?

Earlier in my career, I learned from different mentors in my life and these are a collection of different principles I have developed, perfected and applied in my career. So I decided to pay it forward. I decided I would put them in a book. To give back and provide a tool for others like you to use in your future success.

In this book I have listed 50 simple, yet powerful principles that I believe will take you to a higher performance level in your business, sales, leadership and in your Life. They are all individual principles that are organized in a manner that makes each independent of the others.

You can read or do not need to read in a sequential order. You could just simply flip through to any principles that appeals to you or read them in order either way works.

Some principles will be new to you while others will be a reminder. Some you will easily be able to implement. While others may take little bit of extra effort. Some of these principles will comfort you. While others will change your old paradigm. One thing is for certain, these principles will have you thinking and acting differently. I sincerely hope we can meet in person here in the near future. However, until then it is my great honor to meet you through the pages of this book.

NOTHING IN SALES START UNTIL YOU START

INTRODUCTION

Most people are always striving to better themselves. It's the "American Way". For proof, check the sales figures on the number of self-improvement books sold each year. This is not a pitch for you to jump in and start selling these kinds of books, but it is a indication of people's awareness that in order to better themselves, they have to continue improving their personal selling abilities.

To excel in any selling situation, you must have confidence, and confidence comes, first and foremost, from knowledge. You have to know and understand yourself and your goals. You have to recognize and accept your weaknesses as well as your special talents. This requires a kind of personal honesty that not everyone is capable of exercising.

In addition to knowing yourself, you must continue learning about people. Just as with yourself, you must be caring, forgiving and laudatory with others. In any sales effort, you must accept other people as they are, not as you would like for them to be. One of the most common faults of sales people is impatience when the prospective customer is slow to understand or make a decision. The successful salesperson handles these situations the same as he would if he were asking a girl for a date, or even applying for a new job.

Learning your product, making a clear presentation to qualified prospects, and closing more sales will take a lot less time once you know your own capabilities and failings, and understand

and care about the prospects you are calling upon.

Our society is predicated upon selling, and all of us are selling something all the time. We move up or stand still in direct relation to our sales efforts. Everyone is included, whether we're attempting to be a friend to a co-worker, a neighbor, or selling multi-million-dollar real estate projects. Accepting these facts will enable you to understand that there is no such thing as a born salesman. Indeed, in selling, we all begin at the same starting point, and we all have the same finish line as the goal - a successful sale.

Most assuredly, anyone can sell anything to anybody. As a qualification to this statement, let us say that some things are easier to sell than others, and some people work harder at selling than others. But regardless of what you're selling, or even how you're attempting to sell it, the odds are in your favor. If you make your presentation to enough people, you'll find a buyer. The problem with most people seems to be in making contact - getting their sales presentation seen by, read by, or heard by enough people. But this really shouldn't be a problem, as we'll explain later. There is a problem of impatience, but this too can be harnessed to work in the salesperson's favor.

Most assuredly, anyone can sell anything to anybody. As a qualification to this statement, let us say that some things are easier to sell than others, and some people work harder at selling than others. But regardless of what you're selling, or even how you're attempting to sell it, the odds are in your favor. If you make your presentation to enough people, you'll find a buyer. The problem with most people seems to be in making contact

- getting their sales presentation seen by, read by, or heard by enough people. But this really shouldn't be a problem, as I will explain later. There is a problem of impatience, but this too can be harnessed to work in the salesperson's favor.

We have established that we're all sales people in one way or another. So whether we're attempting to move up from forklift driver to warehouse manager, waitress to hostess, salesman to sales manager or from mail order dealer to president of the largest sales organization in the world, it's vitally important that we continue learning.

Getting up out of bed in the morning; doing what has to be done in order to sell more units of your product; keeping records, updating your materials; planning the direction of further sales efforts; and all the while increasing your own knowledge---all this very definitely requires a great deal of personal motivation, discipline, and energy. But then the rewards can be beyond your wildest dreams, for make no mistake about it, the selling profession is the highest paid occupation in the world!

Selling is challenging. It demands the utmost of your creativity and innovative thinking. The more success you want, and the more dedicated you are to achieving your goals, the more you'll sell. Hundreds of people the world over become millionaires each month through selling. Many of them were flat broke and unable to find a "regular" job when they began their selling careers. Yet they've done it, and you can do it too!

Remember, it's the surest way to all the wealth you could ever want. You get paid according to your own efforts, skill, and knowledge of people. If you're ready to become rich, then think seriously about selling a product or service (preferably something exclusively yours) - something that you "pull out of your brain"; something that you write, manufacture or produce for the benefit of other people. But failing this, the want ads are full of opportunities for ambitious sales people. You can start there, study, learn from experience, and watch for the chance that will allow you to move ahead by leaps and bounds.

This book will teach you how to be an effective and trustworthy sales person. You will find 50 principles that will definitely make you an extraordinary sales person and achieve more success. Some of these principles in the book may not be new and become just a refresher. However, many of these are new concepts you will enjoy like I have.

You will improve your gross sales, and quite naturally, your gross income and it will all start from YOU. Look them over; give some thought to each of them; and adapt them to your own selling efforts.

PRINCIPLE 1

KNOW YOUR SELLING PRINCIPLES

Not only is it important for a sales person to study and master specific techniques in selling, but it is also important to understand the "why" of that sales technique. That enables you to internalize the information, and then make it your own. We want to share with you specific selling principles that will explain the "why" behind the sales techniques you will be learning. One of the principles that should guide you in your sales career is this: Selling is a process, not an event. Even if your sales cycle is short, it is not an event based on luck; it is a planned process. You are a professional sales person, which means you go into all sales calls prepared.

You should know your sales process and where you are in that process with each of your prospects. You should also know what needs to be done to move to the next step. By following a road map, if you will, you will know what needs to happen to move the decision forward. Do you have a process that you follow every time? Or do you let your prospect move you towards whatever he wants to and hope that he makes a positive buying decision? To be professional in selling, you need to know what the steps are in the purchasing cycle and you need to know how to move someone through those steps. You do not leave it up to chance, but you have a procedure that you follow each and every time. This process will obviously need some flexibility, but it is a routine that you practice and master so that you can make every conversation with a prospect count. Selling should involve a relationship between you and your prospect. You need to take the time to get to know the prospect; what he wants and needs, and why he wants and needs those things.

Selling is not something that you do TO someone. It is something you do WITH someone. As the relationship between the prospect and sales person grow, you learn how you may be able to solve a problem your prospect has with one of your products or services. Selling is also the motivated, energetic, and dynamic seeking of customers or prospects with the intent of addressing their needs.

To become successful at selling, one must develop and demonstrate active listening skills. Without them, it is impossible for a seller to find the customer or prospect's need. A successful seller must also learn how to show confidence in presenting their product or service. In addition, sellers must show a certain level of competency with regard to in-depth product or service details. In other words, sellers rely in the prospect or customer's perception of their excellence and/or their expertise at all times. As sellers, you must also learn how to make exciting "moments of truth" for the customer or prospect, even though chances are slim that they will go through with the order. Selling is, in some way, similar to Marketing. Both of them aims to make all interactions with your company a great experience.

PRINCIPLE 2

BE A PROBLEM SOLVER

This is another crucial principle that every budding sales professional should keep in mind. You make more money solving problems than you do by selling your products or services. When you always sell products instead of solving problems, you create frustration and short-term customers. But when you listen to the prospect and understand their problem, and then offer a solution to that problem, you become extremely valuable to your prospect.

Here's an example: Let's say you saw a prospect while attending a car show. Now you know that this customer must love cars and there's a big chance that he is a car owner himself. You, being a sales professional for a car painting service approaches the prospect and begin to make a sales pitch. Do you think you'll be successful in closing the sale with that prospect? No. Because as it turns out, the prospect is not having any issues with the paint on his car. Instead, his main issue with his car is that it always leaks oil. Now here comes another sales professional who offers car services which specifically addresses oil leaks. He makes a sales pitch to the prospect and successfully closes the sale. Why? Because the second sales professional was able to address a specific problem or need of the prospect.

By solving your prospect's needs, you will be able to get more referrals and more loyal customers. Not only should you learn how to solve a current problem, you must also learn how to anticipate the prospect's needs. Anticipating needs or problems sells more products and satisfies more customers. For example, let's say that you have a prospect who recently bought a car. As an automobile tire salesman, you approach him and begin to make your sales pitch about how great your tires are and how it can prevent dangerous accidental skids. Now here comes a second sales professional who sells oil changing and engine maintenance services. Who do you think has a greater chance of closing the sale? The one who has a greater chance of closing the sale would be the second sales professional, of course. Why? Because tires are the last thing to worry about with a brand new car. The second sales professional was able to anticipate that the first thing car owners must address with a brand new car is engine maintenance and an oil change once they reach their first thousand kilometers. He was able to anticipate that need because he knew that the car is still in its "engine break in" stage.

If customers could solve their own problems, they wouldn't need you. To apply this information today, frame what you sell in terms of solutions and you become an expert in their eyes. You see, you're doing your customer a great service by providing them with the benefits of what you sell. If you are thinking about the money you will make from the sale and what you would do with it, then your chances of closing the sale will significantly decrease. Remember, selling is solving.

PRINCIPLE 3

CUSTOMERS BUY BECAUSE OF THEIR OWN REASONS

If there's one thing about a prospect's mindset that most novice sales professionals forget, it is the fact that prospects purchase for their reasons, not yours. Your reason for selling is probably to make a commission. But the customer purchases for their own reasons, not your reasons. Reasons are defined as motives, feelings, and benefits that move people to take action. Reasons are different from benefits. Remember customers buy for 4 reasons and 4 reasons only. They buy to speed up a process, eliminate pain or create pleasure and they only buy if they like you. You need to ask questions to discover the reasons your prospects may want your product or service. But beware the first time you probe the prospect. You get an answer the person thinks you want to hear. The second time you probe, you will get an answer that someone very near to that person would like to hear. The third time you probe, you may just get the truth. Most people are not trying to be deceitful. They just haven't given much thought to what really is important to them. You see, people purchase for emotional and logical reasons. Your job is to discover both kinds of reasons by asking questions.

Don't you ever get annoyed when sales people in a store approaches you and starts telling you about how great this product is, or how many people are buying it right now? It is most likely that you're annoyed because of two things. The sales person in the store is presenting you a product that you're not even interested in. And most of all, they're presenting you with a product in the most persistent — and extremely annoying — manner. You have no reason to buy that particular product hence the non-interest. The same thing applies with your prospect. They will never, ever buy something without any specific reason. Not unless your prospect is a multi-millionaire and is just splurging cash. And even if the customer is interested in the product and there's probable reason to buy, they won't buy it right away. Why? Well, maybe there's something that's making them hesitate. Maybe they don't like the price or the quality of the product. Quality and Price are both valid reasons to consider before making a purchase.

A skilled sales professional will always try to uncover a need and make the prospect realize that there is indeed a reason for him to buy the service or product. Think of it as making a light bulb go off in the prospect or customer's head when they come to a realization. So how do you uncover a need and make the prospect realize that there's a reason to make the purchase? Well, it all starts by asking questions. Help them find their reason to buy the product or service by asking them questions. As you ask questions, both you and the prospect will realize the need for the service or product and whether there's an urgency to fulfill that need. Once you show your prospect that there's a reason to consider what you're offering, the prospect themselves will be the one to seek you out and ask for your product or service. Uncovering the reason and making the prospect realize that they indeed have a valid reason to go through with the sale is one of the basic skills that you must learn in order to be an extremely successful sales professional.

PRINCIPLE 4

CUSTOMERS BUY WHAT YOUR PRODUCT DOES, NOT THE PRODUCT ITSELF

The second selling principle is this: Prospects don't buy your products and services. They buy what your products and services will do for them. It's true that people have different reasons as in the last principle. But this principle focuses on the benefits they realize as a result of owning the product. If you sell mattresses for example, the benefit might be there's room to stretch or get a good night's sleep. It doesn't matter what you think the benefit of the product is. What matters is what the prospect thinks the benefits are.

So the next time someone asks you, what do you sell? Answer in terms of a benefit instead of a product. Here's an example: Let us say that there are two sales professional attending a mattress convention. A prospect comes to the convention looking for a mattress that will fit him and his wife, and also make sure that he doesn't get any backaches when he wakes up in the morning.

The prospect approaches sales person A and asks him, "What are you selling?" Sales person A then tells the prospect that he sells quality mattresses made of soft fabric and high-quality springs that give that bouncy feel when someone lies down on it. The prospect then approaches sales person B and asks the same thing. Sales person B, however, tells the prospect that he is selling mattresses that offer comfortability, affordability, and quality. The mattress offers comfortability by having quality material which eliminates backaches. Affordability in a sense that the cost to buy and maintain the mattress is extremely low. And lastly, quality since it will not exhibit any wear and tear even with excessive use.

So who do you think the prospect will buy the mattress from? If your answer is sales person B, then you are correct. Why? Because sales person B presented what the product does for the customer instead of what the product is. Leading with what a product does — the benefit — will pique your prospect's interest since he is specifically looking for those benefits. Not only will you attract more prospects by leading with the benefit or your product or service, but also increase your chances of closing the sale significantly. Again, why your prospect wants the particular product is uncovered by asking questions. If a customer or a prospect comes to you and asks, "What do you sell?" Ask them a qualifying question first. Ask them why they need that product or service, and then relate the need with your product's benefits.

In order to implement this principle today, concentrate on why your prospects want your products, and what benefits they may derive from it. Both of these answer are found by asking prospecting questions. Do not be afraid to ask your prospect questions. Because only with questions do you find the prospect's reason to buy and make them realize the urgency at which they need to get the product. Remember, lead with the need and sell with great speed.

PRINCIPLE 5

SELL WITH HONESTY AND INTEGRITY

Over the years, sales people have been given a bad rap of being dishonest and unethical. A truly professional sales person, with their goal on a long-term career in sales, realize that honesty; ethical dealings with others is the only way to build a solid career. We hear story after story of people who did the right thing, and were rewarded for it somewhere down the line.

We are also reminded of a sales manager who sent out an inexperienced sales person. The rookie came back with a $225 check for what should have been $125. The manager, of course, quickly took the rookie back to the customer, explained the mistake, and then offered to give them the service for free. The man gladly accepted the offer and then went on to sign up for a $100 monthly service contract.

Now if the manager had not rectified the first mistake of $225, the customer probably would have done some shopping around and found someone more reasonable to give his $1200 a year business to. In the long run, it pays to be honest and straightforward with your prospects and customers. Being ethical is not only the right way to live, it is also the most pragmatic way to live.

A true sales professional not only talks about ethics, he or she also lives ethically. In this day and age, people are searching for people they can trust. Because it is a cynical time, you have to understand that most of the people you deal with for the first time have their guard up. They want to make sure that you can be trusted. This is when a sterling reputation can help you out. You can give references of other customers that will attest to your honesty and your honest way of doing business. And because you have confidence in your product and possess the knowledge that you conduct your life in a fair and honest nature, you could look that prospect right in the eye and exude the warmth and assurance that you are to be trusted. Now, to make use of this technique today, go to the nearest mirror, take a look at it and say, "I am an ethical salesperson. I deal with all people in an honest way."

Repeat this affirmation for the next 30 days and you will increase your feelings of integrity and that will be communicated through your words and your actions. Whatever way you convey your trust, know that you will always come out in the long run better by dealing with everyone you encounter in an honest and ethical manner. As a sales professional, looking to make an illustrious career, it is of utmost importance that you maintain a reputation of trustworthiness. Show people that you can be trusted and you can bet your bottom dollar that the prospects or customers will seek you out themselves. If you have a flawless reputation, they will seek you out by name and always come to you every time they need to product or service that could help them in taking care of a problem.

PRINCIPLE 6

BE POSITIVE THINKER

Unfortunately, there is a lot of confusion about positive thinking. Some people say, "..with a positive attitude you can just do anything." That simply is not true. It won't let you do anything, but it will let you do everything better than negative thinking will.

Here is one simple example. Kobe Bryant is a great athlete. But even with his athleticism, and even if he was a great positive thinker, he still would make a terrible horse jockey. No. We're talking about positive thinking based on specific reasons for that optimistic hope. It is ridiculous and frustrating for a new salesperson to have his manager say, "go get `em." or "I know you can do it" and then send them out with no training or direction.

That leads to frustration and failure. The student must be a constant learner. Preparation will develop a positive attitude to go out and succeed. Remember, your business is never good or bad. It is either good or bad between your own two ears. There are many examples of sales people who are very successful in what is supposedly a down market; a sluggish industry. Don't listen to the naysayers. Keep your attitude up and your sales will follow. There are three action steps you can take:

1. Accept the fact that only you can control your attitude. Your attitude is not governed by the prospect of the manager who does not support you or the economist who predict gloom and doom in your career. You must take

control of your own attitude and develop an optimistic sense of success.

2. Make sure you commit to doing whatever is necessary to keep in control of your attitude. Saying positive affirmations, taking a brisk walk around the block, or whatever steps that work for you to maintain or regain your commitment to taking control counts.

3. Read something of value to you personally and professionally for at least 20 minutes every day. Read something that inspires or educate.

These simple steps will help you keep your attitude in the right frame of mind so that you can be free to be a problem solver for your prospects. If your prospect says NO, don't take it personally. Be a positive thinker and think that maybe the reason why the prospect said no is because he is currently encountering financial issues. If so, present him with payment terms that will ease not add to his financial burden. If the prospect keeps on hesitating to finalize the order, be a positive thinker and think maybe the reason for the stall is because he doesn't have enough information yet to go through the closing of the sale. Never take things personally. If a prospect rejects your offer, know that he or she is rejecting it not because of you, but because he has not realized that he needs the product yet. Be enthusiastic each time you approach a prospect, even though you have been rejected countless times by that same prospect. Once you master the art of thinking positive, you will exude confidence in every sales call.

PRINCIPLE 7

DON'T BE AFRAID OF REJECTION

Research has shown that 63% of all sales interviews end with no direct effort to close the sale. The sales person is comfortable building rapport, asking questions to find the need, and even presenting the offer. But because of a fear of rejection, they talk and talk but never ask for the order. Are you a professional sales person, or are you a professional visitor? Those sales people who have a poor attitude about themselves will have to admit that they have a hard time facing up to rejection. After making a rather spectacular presentation, you find yourself out on the street with no order, no signed paperwork, and nothing to show for your efforts. Those with a bad attitude about themselves will have to go to the closest coffee shop and lick their wounds and have a pity party about how cruel the world can be.

However, those with a healthy attitude will find themselves out on the street after a NO, shake it off, and go about finding the next prospect. This also relates to positive thinking. When you get rejected, think positive and move on to the next prospect. There is a direct bearing over a sales person's self image and their self success. Sales people who have a healthy self image; not conceited but a healthy self-acceptance of their own faults, their shortcomings, and their own strengths can go from one prospect to the next many times and almost regardless of the reception they get. However, let's admit it. There's a limit to how much rejection anyone can stand. The point is, never ever let rejection pull you down.

When you improve your attitude about yourself, in other words improve your self-image, you will improve your sales performance. In order to effectively make use of this today, work on developing and maintaining a healthy attitude about you. There are many ways you can accomplish this task. Here are two action steps that you can take:

1. Dress the part - It is proven that we feel better about ourselves when we are dressed for success. Make sure you are putting your best foot forward by keeping your shoes shined, your hair neat, and your clothes spick and span. Surely you're not expecting a prospect to trust a salesperson who looks like they just jumped out of a dumpster. Always dress like a professional; that you're a well-respected, trusted salesperson.

2. Become an expert in your chosen profession of selling. Learn the sales techniques that work best in your selling situation. Practice them until they become a part of you. With improved effectiveness, your love for selling would be even greater, because an important key to maintaining a good attitude is to know what you are doing. Besides, no prospect would trust a sales person who does not know the Do's and Dont's of selling. Learn your craft and learn it well. Become a master of your field; an expert. We all know that everybody runs to the expert if things go sour.

PRINCIPLE 8

GIVE IMPORTANCE TO THE CUSTOMER

How do you really view the person you're dealing with across the desk, the conference table, or the phone? Is he just another someone you can make a buck by selling to? Or does he represent a person with a problem which you can help solve? Are you really focused on him? Or in making the sale and spending the commission?

In survey after survey, the number one complaint from customers is that of rudeness, inefficiency, or just plain indifference. Two of these have to do with simple human relations; how we feel. Our attitude about our prospects and customers come out loud and clear in our actions.

The Forum Corporation studied high and low performance sales people. One of their discoveries was that the high performing sales people took just as much time and effort with their internal customer--those inside their organization--as with their external customers. Most sales people's success depends upon people to whom they have little or no supervisory control. High performing sales people understand that respect and a positive attitude towards those in shipping, installation, service and administration will help them please the external customer, and possibly lead to more sales and referrals.

You see, making a serious effort to keep our customers makes good economic sense. It costs more to bring in a new customer than it does to keep a current customer. It costs more time, effort, as well as marketing dollars. Also, if that customer leaves disgruntled, he'll tell an average of 11 other people about the problem he had with you and your organization. What most novice sales professionals fail to realize is that it will take more time and effort to appease a disgruntled customer than to develop and maintain a good relationship with one. This is the reason why companies spend millions of dollars in customer retention via their customer service department.

So a high performing sales person does not think in terms of replacing customers. Instead, he or she thinks in terms of maintaining customers and adding new ones in order to build his or her business bigger and better. In order to be a successful sales person, be sensitive to the value of the customer's time. Because you've spent more time planning your strategy and preparing for the call, spend more quality time in front of the customer.

Customers perceive this and will value it highly. Become aware of the personal pressures and needs faced by the customers and sell the people, not the company. Take time to build relationships with both your internal and external customers. Relationships are what makes a customer come back to you again and again to buy more products or services. If the customer encounters problems at any stage of the sales process, be quick to come to their rescue and help them move towards completing the sales. Show the prospect or customer that they are important no matter the size of the business pie they are bringing into your company.

PRINCIPLE 9

DEVELOP A PROSPECTING ATTITUDE

No matter how good you are at building rapport, uncovering needs and wants, asking questions, asking for the order, managing objections, making your presentation or your product knowledge, you're out of business if you do not have a prospect. Prospecting is one of the most important keys to your success. So when should you be prospecting? Well, the answer is all the time.

Prospecting is not an eight to five job. Prospecting when performed amicably, can be done in essentially any setting; in social gatherings, at an airport, on an airplane, at a club meeting or during lunchtime. I call this "B.A.M." (Be Always Marketing). In general, wherever people are present is an opportunity to prospect. This does not necessarily mean you approach everyone at the party, or corner the people on the driving range, or speak to every person at the post office, or in line at the fast food place.

The successful prospecting attitude does mean, however, that when great prospectors pick up the newspaper, there is a sensitivity to local events or news stories that contain leads or prospects for the business. The successful prospecting attitude means tuning in to conversations that would directly, or indirectly, involve the use of the product or service you offer. Pay attention to the events, trends, conversations, and your current customers. Regularly get out of the networking circles you're in and start another circle or chain. Don't let your courier depend on one specific group of individuals. How do you prospect? First, you must develop a genuine interest in other people. Open up a friendly conversation about something you're both experiencing and begin listening to the other person. In the conversation, you may find out that you have a product or service they would need, or at least get a chance to tell them what you do.

In another section, you will discover a way, in a quick sentence or two, to pique someone's interest. Have you ever had the experience that when you bought a certain car, say a red Ford, and then wherever you look you saw red Fords? It's the same thing with prospecting. If you're thinking about prospects and looking for them wherever you go, you will surely find them.

To be an effective prospector, make it a point to speak to at least two new people that you don't know. Strike up a conversation and see where it leads you. It will take some practice to become comfortable and effective at this, but what a great benefit to have a full pipeline of prospects. Having a stable pipeline of prospects allows you to focus on spending time with them and addressing their need, instead of spending countless hours or even days looking for one. Always find opportunities to discuss your business without coming off as being too pushy or suggestive. Remember, every person you encounter is an opportunity for you to not only to help them with a need, but also to develop a long lasting relationship. One that could prove beneficial to both you and your customer.

PRINCIPLE 10

LEARN HOW TO FIND OUT YOUR FINEST LEAD SOURCES

Prospects come from many lead sources. It is important that you know your best lead sources. Some categories include:

1. Existing customers - These are the people whom you are currently dealing with. The usual question that comes into mind when dealing with existing customers is, are they willing to buy more or different products from you? This is considered as one of the best sources of leads. Since they already bought a product or service from you, you've already built rapport with these customers and it only takes a slight shove in the right direction for them to make another purchase.

2. Referrals - These are a great lead source because you go into the process with an introduction from someone else. These usually come from existing customers, or past customers who no longer need your services or products, but knows a friend, a colleague, or a family member who does.

3. A warm market - This is your family, your friends, your colleagues, former customers; people you know personally and have already developed a rapport and trust. This is usually the lead source most novice sales professionals take their prospects from. The reason being is that since you already developed rapport and trust,

the chances of them buying from you is high.

4. A niche market or related industry - This is a business that you are competing against, but is what you sell into. In other words, you and the sales person at that business can team up to offer an excellent full service package. Of course, you may be lucky enough to work for a business that has a marketing effort that generates leads for you. Think of this as having a symbiotic relationship with competition.

5. Cold calling - This is done best through your observation of new business openings in newspaper articles, or other current events. But sometimes, it is just getting a list of people and starting to dial the phone.

Of all these lead sources, which are the ones that work best for you? To be able to find out your finest lead sources, write down on a piece of paper the six categories that we have mentioned and estimate the percentage of your prospects that come from each of those sources. 35% of most sales people's prospects come from existing customers, 15% through referrals, 5% through what we call "warm" market, 5% through a niche market, 30% through their marketing efforts, and 10% through cold calls that they make. By doing this on your own, you can find out your situation and you can see where your prospects are coming from. Now realize that not all of these categories give you qualified prospects.

So identify which categories are at the top; those that you can turn prospects into qualified buyers and into customers. In order to grow your business, you must handle your leads or your prospects efficiently. The point is to invest time and effort on the prospects that yield you the highest returns.

> "TO EXCEL IN ANY SELLING SITUATION, YOU MUST HAVE CONFIDENCE, AND CONFIDENCE COMES, FIRST AND FOREMOST, FROM KNOWLEDGE"

PRINCIPLE 11

KNOW EXACTLY WHAT A PROSPECT IS?

All throughout this book, we will mentioned the word "prospect" countless times. So the question is, what is a prospect? We ask the question because there is a difference between a "suspect" and a "prospect." Suspects have the potential to be prospects. But you don't know yet. A prospect has a need for the product, a possible desire to own the product, and the financial capability to implement that decision. Remember this: You spend time with suspects; you invest time with prospects.

Right now, our goal is to create a profile of your ideal prospect so that you can identify the characteristics and demographics surrounding those that you have already closed, and then look for similar entities to do business with. For example, if within your existing customer-base your best customers are in a certain geographical area, you owe it to yourself to explore other opportunities in the same geographic area.

The same will hold true if they belong to a trade association. Everyone else in that association would be a warm market for you. Taking the time to find this information is important. So, what does the ideal prospect look like for you? To create this profile, you begin to think about your current customers. What similarities can you see in them? Do they have the same job title? Or are they from the same industry? Are they companies? All about the same size or location? Don't forget, when you are building the profile of this ideal prospect, you must consider the company as well as yourself. Would this type of customer be the most profitable to the company? Or for you to have a sale? You need to make sure you are targeting the customers who give you the best return on your time invested. Once you identify a prospect that fits the profile of a good customer of yours, you must contact that prospect with the intention of asking enough questions so that you can either:

1. Turn them from a suspect to a prospect, or
2. Disqualify them as a prospect, ad them to your "Drip List" to follow up later and move on, or
3. Find the real buyer or decision maker, or
4. Sell your Products

Keep in mind that a truly qualified prospect should meet all these qualifications. They have the authority to buy, the ability to pay, and an unmet need. It is important not to push products on people who are not qualified prospects. It wastes time and damages their trust in you and your company. It's better to disqualify a prospect and move on. To better identify the qualified prospect, create a profile of your best customer and begin to look for prospects that fit that profile. Realize that there are some prospects who buy that don't fit that profile. Use the profile as a sort of magnifying glass to zero in on the best people to spend your time with. Even if you think that you have the best product or service in the world, there are people out there who couldn't care less. Your job is to eliminate them quickly so you can help the people who do need what you sell. If you keep eliminating the NO's, you have more time for the YES's.

PRINCIPLE 12

LEARN HOW TO USE ELEVATOR STATEMENTS

When you get the familiar question, "What do you do?", how do you answer? If you answer with a job description like, "Oh, I'm in sales for the Excelsior Company," then you are not using that opportunity to prospect. What you want is a statement that makes the listener intrigued, and is prompted to ask you more. These statements are basically called elevator statements. The reason why they are called as such is because they have to be fast enough, and noteworthy enough to pique someone's interest in the time it takes to ride an elevator. A good statement needs to be short, about a key benefit, and said with sincerity. If you have limited time with someone, it will help you establish credibility quickly and hopefully get the potential prospect interested to hear more. Some examples of elevator statements are:

- What do you do? I build better business by building better individuals.

- What do you do? We provide the keys to the American dream of owning a home.

- What do you do? We work with clients that have a passion to increase their business while creating more family time.

Each of these examples give just enough information for the prospect to want to know how or why or what you're talking about. You use elevator statements if you're meeting someone in a quick setting; an airport, a chamber of commerce meeting, or any place that you can get the question, "What do you do?" To effectively pique your prospects interest, brainstorm some quick, clever statements that describe what you do in terms of a benefit. To do that, ask yourself what you like best about the product, the service, or the company you work for. It's a good place to begin describing your job in terms of what you can do for others.

One of the National Guard recruiters was asked what he does for a living. And he said that he helps young people attain their dreams. That reply would certainly get a conversation going. It will allow the recruiter to expand on the benefits of college tuition, paid training, and many other benefits of joining the U.S. Army National Guard. Create two or three of these elevator statements and practice using them to become comfortable and effective at using every opportunity as a prospecting opportunity. By now, it would have dawned on you that the key to prospecting is learning how to hook the prospect in; raising their curiosity about you and what you have to offer. The elevator statement is designed to do just that.

Once you hook the prospect in, you have every opportunity to probe and uncover their need, and present the benefit of the product or service that you are offering in relation to that need. And with a little bit of objection handling skills--if there are any objections by the prospect at all — you will surely convince the prospect that they indeed need what you are offering. Once the groundwork has been laid, you can now ask to close the sales.

PRINCIPLE 13

LEARN HOW TO USE GENERAL BENEFIT STATEMENTS

When you want to capture the attention of a prospect, you can use a general benefit statement. Now this statement is longer than the elevator statement that we just finished discussing. It is used when you are calling on a list of people in which you want to generate interest in talking to further. It is also when you call and leave a voicemail message. Now this statement will increase your chances of a successful first contact. It will also give the prospect a reason for meeting or talking with you. In other words, it creates value. General benefit statements include three parts: your competitive advantage, a sales objective, and a brief information point about the prospect.

Your competitive advantage is a benefit that your product or service has over the competition. While you don't know this prospect yet, or if this benefit is specific to the prospect, you do know that it is a general benefit that most prospects are drawn to. So you need to do some thinking, some research, and some comparison to your competition. What does your product or service have that others don't have? Is your warranty better? Or does your product save more time? Does it have less maintenance cost? Or does your company provide superior technical follow-up, better service, or cheaper installation?

This competitive advantage is a great way to leverage yourself into an appointment with that prospect. Once you get to know the prospect's situation a little better, you can then target the features and benefits that fit directly to the prospect. For now, you are just trying to win the opportunity to talk further with the person. Next, you want to state your objectives to the prospect clearly. It could be many things. For instance, you may be calling to secure an appointment, introduce your new product, or set a follow-up phone call. You need to know why you're calling them so the prospect can know why you're calling. The last part of your statement is to let the prospect know that you've done a little research and you know a little about him or her. Give the feeling that you're interested enough to have done some homework. If you're reaching the prospect for the first time, say something like this:

"Hello Mr. Smith. My name is Jason Webber. I represent the Chicago Marketing Initiative. I'm calling because the Bellagio is very similar to another hotel property in Chicago that we've been helping to increase their guest retention. Recently, this client has realized that there's a 37% increase in return customers using our program. Now, since you're the director of guest services at the Bellagio, I assume that you're under constant competitive pressure, is that right? If there were a way I could help you relieve that pressure, would you be interested in meeting with me? Well, that's great. I think a 20 minute appointment would be a perfect starting point to see if what we offer is something your hotel could use to increase your occupancy.

I'm open on Mondays or Wednesdays. Which would work for you?"

PRINCIPLE 14

LEARN HOW TO DO PIPELINE PLANNING

Successful sales professionals understand that having prospects to call on is an important part of the selling cycle. This process is called "Pipeline planning." Having a steady supply of leads based on probability of "close" ensures the sales professional is managing the future as well as the present. Pipeline planning requires understanding and categorizing your prospects by metrics that are important to you and your business. It would need to include name, primary contact, contact information, probability of close, and type of customer; either new or existing. Take your current prospects and list them on paper. The probability of close could mean you would put an "A" beside a prospect that you think would close in less than 30 days. A "B" based on the probability you will close in less than 60 days. And a "C" based on thinking the close will happen in less than 90 days.

You can adjust the timeline to fit your specific situation or selling cycle. This list, when filled out, would give you an opportunity to look at a projection of your activities and ensure that you have enough qualified leads to work on every single day.

There's all kinds of software out there that can keep all pertinent information, or you could do what every successful salesman did before these software advancements came to be; they took an old-fashioned 3x5 card, wrote their top 20 accounts on it, then worked on those accounts until they said no or wrote up the order. As soon as one prospect closed and became a customer, they would erase the name and replace it. It was low-tech, but it kept them focused on what they needed to do on any given day.

Do you go to work every day with a clear plan of what must be done to close business already in the cycle? Do you know the activities that need to be done to replace that prospect when you close the sale? If the answer is NO, then write down your current pipeline on paper or put one into your computer today. This is the first step to jumpstarting your activity and ultimately your success. Remember, an organized sales person is an efficient sales person. If you don't manage your pipeline properly, there's a big probability that you'll lose track of a potential customer. Unless you have a secretary who handles everything for you--which you probably don't since you're a budding sales professional reading this book--you have to develop a system that allows you to keep track of who's who. Always find ways of streamlining your pipeline handling process. Go old-school if you have to. But do not let your Pipeline become disorganized.

Think of your pipeline as the life blood that allows you to live. If you're bleeding all over the place, chances are high that you'll die due to loss of blood. Same principle applies in sales. If you're pipeline is disorganized, you can be rest assured that your business will soon die.

PRINCIPLE 15

LEARN HOW TO DO PIPELINE MANAGEMENT

When you are under pressure to make your quota, it's easy to concentrate only on the closing end of the sales process. However, you have to continually have new prospects to talk to if you want to continue to make your sales quota. You need to manage your pipeline of prospects so that at all times, you have prospects moving through each step of your sales process. If you don't, then you will have dry spells and a certain drop in revenue.

Managing this process is called "Pipeline Management." It requires that you not only keep the pipeline flow by prospecting, but that for each stage of your sales cycle, you identify clearly what activities need to be accomplished for that prospect to turn into a customer. If you're managing your pipeline, then you will have better sales forecasting and you will know what you need to do daily to keep the revenue up.

Too much attention to any step of the sales cycle--for instance closing activities--will mean not enough attention somewhere else--for instance prospecting. And there will be a constant need to play catch-up somewhere. That can be draining to your mental, as well as your physical health. The trick is to balance your activities between the prospects who are in the beginning stages of the sales cycle and those who are in the closing stages of the sales cycle.

It is best to setup some accountability checkpoints. These are regular scheduled times that you review your pipeline with your manager or yourself. Technology can certainly automate some of this information so that you can quickly look and see what activities need to be accomplished with what prospect and when. CRM or Customer Relationship Management software is easily found. And investing your time in learning this software will pay off as it frees you up to do what you do best, namely sell.

To be able to successfully manage your pipeline, you need not only have a forum created for your pipeline, review it regularly, and then plan your daily, weekly, and monthly sales activities with that information. Knowing this information is critical to your success. An unmanaged pipeline is a dead pipeline. It is important to keep the flow of prospects moving along the sales process. If for example you find that most of your prospects become stuck at the order fulfillment stage of the sales process, be quick to find the root cause of the problem, address it with the appropriate department in your company, and keep the sales process going alone. This will sure make your customers happy. And we all know that a happy customer will always return again to do business. As you can see it all relates to keeping a fine lead source and making your customers feel like they are the most important people in the world for you. And because of this, they will trust you more. Strengthening the bond between customer and seller should be always your end-game.

PRINCIPLE 16

DEMONSTRATE YOUR INTENT AND DESIRE TO HELP

Sales managers and sales professionals often get caught up in the sales skills trap in an attempt to find the secret or missing ingredient to their sales process. They focus on sales techniques, when in fact they should be focused on intent. As what many successful sales veterans say, you can have everything in this life that you want as long as you help enough people to get what they want.

The goal of a true selling professional is to help their prospects and their customers get what they want. And more importantly, what they need. The key is to remember that intent is more important than technique. In other words, your desire to help is far more important than knowing fourteen different ways to close a sale. So how do we demonstrate our desire and out intent to help our prospects and customers? Well, for starters, try this. Before launching into your probing questions to uncover any need for your product or service, begin by framing the sales call. After the warm-up or initial small talk and greetings, try something like this:

"Thank you again for your time today and for having us here. We really have a simple agenda for today's meeting. First, we would like to know more about you, your role and some of the projects and initiatives you're currently working on. Secondly, we will share a little bit about ourselves; the company and what we do. And lastly, if it's appropriate and make sense, we can look together at action items or next steps. Does that sound fair?"

More than likely, your prospect or customer will say, "Yes. Of course, it sounds fair." They may add to the agenda or do a time check, but they will usually agree that it's a fair way to begin a meeting. Now, let's analyze the wording. You ask permission to learn more about them, then share a little about you. More them, little you.

Then you use the words "we," "us," and "together." When they agree that the agenda sounds fair, they have agreed to allow you to ask questions first and learn more about them. By asking relevant questions and taking the time to understand their business needs, you'll have moved from a vendor relationship to more of a partner or consulting relationship. This path will certainly help you demonstrate your intent and desire to help your prospects and customers find the solutions they truly need.

Once you've expressed your sincerest intent and desire to help them address an ongoing or impending issue, then they'll be more interested on what you have to say about how your product or service can benefit them. To implement this technique successfully, write down the sentences we used previously to frame the sales call on an index card. Review it until you can say it conversationally and comfortably. You will find that people are interested in talking about themselves and their situations, which then gives you the information you need to help solve their problems. Express your intent, uncover their need, and then close the sale.

PRINCIPLE 17

LEARN HOW TO OVERCOME CALL RELUCTANCE

Have you ever felt anxious before making a sales call? If you're human, then the answer is probably, YES. The difference between the sales person that is struggling to get by and the successful sales person is the ability to direct that nervous energy. As a matter of fact, if you feel no anxiety in making the sales call, your chances of success will go down. Realizing that your anxiety is a positive factor, not a negative one, allows you to focus on the most important factor in call reluctance; that's YOU.

According to sales experts, 84% of all sales people have call reluctance to some degree. This fear is manifested in a thousand different ways. But procrastination is the number one indicator that a problem is developing. When you create non-essential tasks that must be done before talking to a prospect, call reluctance is setting in. We would like to share with you three ideas to overcome call reluctance.

The first idea is realize that selling is a transference of feeling. If you transfer the feeling that you must make the sale for your benefit, the chances of making the sale are greatly reduced. If you transfer the feeling that you want to make the sale for the prospect's benefit, your chances for success are dramatically increased. Take the focus off of you and your nervousness, and mentally put the focus on helping the prospect solve their problem.

The second idea is to use the experimental syndrome to overcome feelings of rejection, by making each call a positive experiment instead of a negative experience. In your mind, turn each sales call into an experience, instead of an experiment. The experimental syndrome basically works like this: Every time you come up to a customer or a prospect, whether face-to-face or via telephone, you must keep in mind that you're just doing an experiment that aims to find out how the prospect will react towards you.

Document all the prospect's responses with a simple chart. When you approach your target, instead of taking his or her reaction personally, simply jot down all the reactions that you've observed. This way, the prospect's actions towards you will have a minimal effect. Your focus and concentration are not "the experience, but instead they are on "the experiment." Remember that you're the good guy in this picture. The vile prospect or customer is the one with problem. Push through with your experiment and let them dwell on their problem. The best part out of all of these is that as you become accustomed and adapt to many different prospect reactions, you will have a great confidence boost and become even more effective and efficient in your approach and presentation.

The last idea is to get on a recurrent timetable and make an engagement with yourself to be face to face with a qualified prospect at the same time every day. It is important to get on an organized program, followed in a disciplined manner. No matter what small obstacles that try to get in your way at the exact same time every day, you are face to face with a prospect. There's a simple, yet profound psychological reason that this works, and it is the fact that logic will not change an emotion, but action will. Call reluctance is not something that is consistently overcome with logic since it is an emotion. Get into action, support the action with logic and sales success is sure to be yours.

> "EVERY NEW CONTACT YOU MEET CAN BECOME LONG-TERM POSSIBILITIES FOR SALES OR NETWORKING"

PRINCIPLE 18

LEARN HOW TO MAKE A POSITIVE FIRST IMPRESSION

People, including your prospects and customers, will take from 3 to 30 seconds to make a decision about whether they want to give you their time and attention. Once the impression has been made, all the information will be filtered through that initial decision. How can you and your company make a positive first impression, and then build on that to establish trust and rapport? Let's first look at your company. When someone is coming to your establishment to do business, what do they see? They begin to form opinions about your business before they talk to a single person.

Is the building neat and clean? Is the reception area projecting the right image for your business? Take a look around; your physical surroundings through the eyes of the prospect. Is it making the best first impression? Maybe your prospect's first contact with your company is over the phone. Is it answered properly? Do they have to go through a series of impersonal voicemail options before getting to a live person? Maybe your prospect's first contact is through the mail. Are your company's marketing pieces professional? Are they well written and well designed? You may have little or no input into how your company forms an impression for the prospect. So, let's turn our attention onto what you can control--YOU personally.

How do you create a positive first impression? Just as a prospect may make an impression of your business from the outside people, we'll also form an impression of you based on your "outside." Are you clean, neat, warm, and friendly? Think about your business card. When you hand it to someone, does it make the right impression? Keep the design simple. Use the front of your card to display your contact information only. Use the back of the card to give your company's mission statement, a map to your office, a list of products and services you can offer, anything that is helpful to the prospect.

But, beware. As important as first impressions can be, the most current contact the person has had with you or your company will be the freshest thing on their minds. So start strong with a positive first impression, but remain strong with consistent follow-up, attention to service, and a focus on solving the prospect's needs and wants. To be able to make a first impression right now, take inventory of all the opportunities you have to contact a prospect, you physical building, your marketing materials, your business card, and the most important, YOU the sales person. What kind of impression are you making? What can you do to improve the impression you are making? Strive to make the best impression possible as you know people like to buy from people they trust. Make every effort to express your sincere trustworthiness and you will make a positive lasting impression. Remember, good impressions is what makes a recurring customer. The good about a recurring customer is that you don't have to look for them. They will be the one to proactively look for you and give you their business.

PRINCIPLE 19

ALWAYS BE A 'CURIOUS' QUESTIONER

Questions allow us to gather information which enables us to help our clients. And just as important is when we ask questions in a professional manner. By asking questions in a professional manner, we establish the most important thing in the sales process; trust. When you ask questions in a sincere manner, then you show that you are truly interested in the prospect's best interest.

Properly worded questions are the best way to discover the true needs of a prospect or client. Questions demonstrate that the purpose of our call is to find the prospect's needs and interest while gathering information. So that together we can learn how our products and services can benefit their needs. Prospects like to be heard in order to have the confidence that you really do understand that their situation is different. In reality, their situation may not be different. But reality, like beauty, is in the eye of the beholder.

We can never gain the trust of prospects until they believe we are really interested in solving their "unique" problem. We are not suggesting that you ask a series of questions that feels like an interrogation; or questions so obvious that you are leading them down a specific path. Instead, what we're suggesting is that you ask questions that combine both the emotion and the logic. Use thinking and feeling questions. Questions phrased with, "How do you feel about it?" will help you learn how the customer feels. And then you are more likely to find out what that person thinks.

There are two aspects of the mind that you want to combine; logic and emotion. The one that prompts the prospect to make that buying decision is emotion. Logic, on the other hand, allows them to make that justification on the purchase that they've made afterwards. Be sure to ask more open-ended questions than close-ended questions. Open-ended questions are those most valuable types of questions that you can ask. Because they allow the prospect to give you the most information about themselves and their issues. They begin with words like, "What," "How," "Why," "When," or "Tell me more about that." Now close-ended questions can be answered with a simple yes or no. Use them to gather facts. They should be used infrequently during the sales process.

You can also ask reflective questions. They give you a chance to reflect on a previous comment and give the prospect a chance to elaborate on clarity. A question that begins with, "What do you mean by...?" or "How is that impacting your business?" are examples of follow-up questions to the prospect's previous answer. You will also want to occasionally use a direct agreement question. Now these are yes-no-type answered questions, but you know the answer before you ask them. For example, "This would save you time, wont it?" This gets the prospect into an agreeing mode. The agreeing mode helps you sell later on. To apply these types of questions properly, write down sample questions you could use with your next prospect or customer. Then work some of those questions into your conversations to see how they can work for you. You can benefit from being curious and asking more questions, can't you?

PRINCIPLE 20

LEARN TO LISTEN UP

Asking your prospects or customers questions about what their desires and needs are, is just not enough. It is also crucial that you focus and listen to what they are saying. Have you ever heard of a sales person miss a sale because he or she listened intensely to a customer or prospect's wants, needs, and desires? Of course not. In fact, the more information you have about the customer's needs, the better positioned you are in satisfying those needs. In addition, the trust factor between you and your prospect goes up. Every time the prospect or customer sees that you are listening attentively to their desires and needs, they have a greater chance of giving you their trust. However, listening is not a piece of cake, especially if you're eager about what you are offering and want the customer or prospect to hear all the important and great features that your product has. Nevertheless, know that in order for you to succeed in sales, listening is an absolute must.

Listening is a kind of mental discipline. You have to curb your desire to utilize the time when the customer or prospect is talking, as the time to prepare what it is that you are going to say next. It is not appropriate to let your mind drift to other things while a person of interest is talking. Listening is also a kind of physical discipline. There are things your body can do to help your mind to listen intensely. Making eye contact, leaning forward, making a nodding gesture, are just some actions your body can take to assist your mind in listening closely to the prospect or customer. When you listen, listen with more than just your ears. Learn to listen with your eyes as well. In other words, look out for numerous non-verbal indicators that give insight to the customer or prospect. Sometimes, we get overly excited about presenting what we have to offer that we continue to talk and talk about us instead if listening to them. Not listening intently to the prospect is a rookie mistake that every sales professional must learn to avoid at all cost. Never ever make the prospect feel that you're not interested in what he or she has to say, or is disregarding his or her insights.

Observe how your prospect stands or sits. Watch how they frown or smile. Look for everything and anything that would give you an indication of their frame of mind at that specific point in time. Take note of how fast the person is speaking, apart from his or her voice's intonation and intensity. You must also learn to empathetically listen to your prospect or customer. Always put yourself in the prospect's shoes; how would you feel if you were in his or her situation. Always listen with an open heart. Do this as you take note of the specific words your prospect uses, and his or her emotional involvement with those words. Lastly, always remember not to finish a thought, sentence, or phrase each time your customer or prospect pauses; do not interrupt him or her for whatever reason.

PRINCIPLE 21

LEARN THE P.O.G.O. FORMULA

Sometimes, it feels uncomfortable to fire off a series of questions to prospects you are meeting for the first time. The P.O.G.O. formula will give you a track to run on that doesn't feel like an interrogation. It's a conversational way to ask questions at the beginning of the sales process. You can adapt P.O.G.O. to your own style while you are showing sincere interest in your prospect. These questions are designed to give you a chance to build rapport with the prospect, as well as to begin gathering information on how best to make the sale. While you ask questions, it will be important for you to also talk about yourself and your organization to the extent that you find common ground.

The rule is you should talk about your own P.O.G.O. story only 25% of the time, and let the prospect talk 75% of the time. The letter "P" in the P.O.G.O. formula stands for "Person." You will want to ask questions about the prospect, and the other people involved in the sales process. This makes your prospect feel important. You connect on a personal level. And you show respect for other decision makers while you are designing a series of questions relating to the person. Remember that it is okay to share some personal information about yourself. But you already know about you. Give just enough about yourself to express common interest, but not enough to monopolize the conversation.

Some sample questions you might ask are, "How did you get into this particular business?" or "How long have you been a baseball player?" or "What part of the country do you come from originally?" To work on using these types of questions, you need to write out your list of possible questions, and then practice making them sound conversational. Go as far as to record yourself and ask yourself, "Would I buy for me?"

The first letter "O" in the P.O.G.O. formula stands for "Organization." Ask questions about the organization, department, and team. Learn about the company's structure, decision making process, headquarters, and brand names. Probe gently and be willing to talk about your organization and the places you have positive common ground. Be sensitive to what the prospect wants to know about you and your company. Some prospects are anxious to know about you. And you must give them enough information to build confidence that your company is solid and reputable. However, do not monopolize the conversation. Your objective is to give them enough information to build that confidence, and to gather enough information to make you effective at knowing how to close the sale.

The letter "G" in the P.O.G.O. formula stands for "Goals." This is the time for gathering information about personal and professional goals such as, "What do you want to attain in the coming months?" and "What goals do you have in place for the next year?" The second letter "O" in the P.O.G.O. formula stands for "Obstacles." Ask about what must be overcome in order to reach the goals. This is where you start to get an idea of what problems they face for which you may have a solution. You can ask, "Would you be willing to share some of the problems your organization faces?" or "What is holding you back from being at the top?"

"Remember, the surest way to all the wealth is too be inquisitive"

PRINCIPLE 22

LEARN TO ASK QUESTIONS EFFECTIVELY TO UNCOVER THE NEED

Have you ever seen cartoons where the character get's an idea, and suddenly a light bulb pops up above his head? This means that he is now aware of something he didn't know before. As you move from building trust and rapport with the P.O.G.O. questions that was previously discussed, you are now trying to identify the prospect's needs.

This is also achieved through the art of asking specific questions. During this stage in the sales cycle, it is important for both you and the prospect to be fully aware of his needs. This is critical before you start to sell a solution. Imagine a light bulb indicating need awareness that has suddenly illuminated above your head as you ask him questions. Because you've now begin to uncover and understand his needs. By asking the right questions, you will uncover needs of which he was not aware. You might say to yourself that now you understand what he's trying to say, or understand what he needs. If you don't have this awareness, you don't know what to recommend. You can't move to the solution step until you have clearly determined in your mind what the prospect needs.

You are better able to identify a need and offer the solution when you are an expert in your own product, you have pricing knowledge, industry knowledge, and competitor knowledge. As the saying goes, "Knowledge is power." The more you know about your offering, the easier it is to see how it can solve the needs your prospects have. The more you know before you begin your sales presentation, the better armed you are to tailor your offering to specifically what the prospect needs.

A common mistake is for sales people to probe for needs, discover one, and take-off in solving the problem. All before the prospect has decided it is indeed a need he has. Not only must the light bulb go off over your head to understand the need, the light bulb must go off over the prospect's head, too. If you tell the prospect that he needs this and that, he will never believe you unless he realizes himself that he indeed need what you have to offer. Until you both clearly have indentified the needs and wants, it is not time to begin showing off your great product. Keep asking questions.

Apply this information today by creating a list of questions that you can use to begin to gently probe for knowledge; the needs that you prospects may have whether they know it or not. Practice these questions with a friend or a colleague. Do a role play and rehearse how you will uncover the need of the prospect, while at the same time making him realize that he indeed needs that product or service. Once you master this art flawlessly, you're chances of getting a YES answer from your prospect will increase. As the saying goes, "It takes two hands to clap." One hand cannot clap by itself. The same principle applies in uncovering the needs of the prospect.

PRINCIPLE 23

LEARN HOW TO UNCOVER THE NEED: THE PROSPECT

Now let's discuss what happens with the prospect during the needs awareness part of the sales cycle. Even when you are sure you have discovered the client's needs, you must continue probing for more information for two basic reasons:

1. To be sure you have the true need and not a symptom of the need.

2. To be sure the prospect understands that there really is a need.

When a skilled sales person, such as yourself, probes with the right questions, the person who may have been denying the problem is permitted to "discover" the problem. Since he discovered it, he would be far more open to discovering solutions. This is where you come in. In order for the prospect to be interested in your solutions, he must be upset with his current condition. He must feel out of balance. The natural law of homeostasis states that an organism stays in balance until and unless an outside force acts upon it. The force causes the status quo to be disrupted, and the organism becomes out of balance. The organism strives to regain balance or get back to status quo. The same is true for your prospects. Once out of balance, they will usually take action to correct the balance.

Human beings don't make changes until they know they're out of balance. We're not saying you should literally knock your prospect out of balance. Instead, you must discover where there is an imbalance and point it out in a convincing manner. In essence, this makes your prospect uncomfortable or unhappy with his condition or situation. Which means you are now in the position to make a sale because your prospect wants to solve his problem. What happens when a prospect becomes imbalanced? Well, there are three things that can happen when customers discover their area of imbalance. In the first place, the professional sales person--YOU--who has helped point out the lack of balance, places the product or service in the hands of the prospect, makes the sale, and now has to worry about how to spend their commissions.

In the second place, the prospect discovers their imbalance and the sales person doesn't ask for the order/sale. Over a period of time, the prospect regains balance and forgets he was ever uncomfortable. This is disastrous because the prospect is not doing very well, and neither are you. In the third place, when the prospect discovers they're out of balance and the sales person doesn't ask for the order, many times the competition comes in and asks for the order, rights of the prospect, and makes the sale. At this point, everyone is happy, but you. It's important that you know how to identify the needs and how to get the prospect to also identify their needs. To be able to make use of this technique effectively, make a list of common areas of imbalance that your product or service can solve. Then develop some specific, pointed questions that you will ask for the prospect to begin to see their needs.

PRINCIPLE 24

LEARN HOW TO MAKE USE OF STATUS QUO QUESTIONS

You have a prospect that seems generally satisfied with his business or his family life. Depending on your sales focus, what can you do to help him feel a need for the solution you want to present to him? In other words, for your product. You may be in a sales situation where people come in with a need already. Your focus is to make sure you understand the need, or help them clarify their real need. Either way, how do you disrupt the status quo? Remember, selling isn't just telling. Selling is asking. A professional sales person knows how to use questions to guide the conversation along. A sales person unsure of himself is afraid to let the prospect speak for fear of never getting the chance to present his solution. But a prospect is less likely to buy if they are not convinced they first have a need. And needs are uncovered with questions. Your questions need to be practiced, drilled, and rehearsed. It is not by accident that a professional sales person gets the prospect to realize they need the service or product being offered. It is with carefully crafted questions that the sales person reaches the goal of a sale. Same example questions that help get the prospect out of status quo are:

- How satisfied are you with your current situation?

- What would you change about your current vendor if you could?

- Are you dissatisfied enough to take action today?

- How has your business changed recently for you to be willing to consider a new solution?

- Would it be helpful to know which other companies in your industry have used our product successfully?

- Have you considered what you would lose if you waited to make a change?

- What is the most important decision you must make before you can decide to make a change?

The more precise the question, the sooner you get the information you need to uncover a need. Many times, sales people attempt to present their solution before the prospect is ready. The only way for you to know if your prospect understands he has a need and feels off balance is by asking smart, well thought out questions. There are times when a prospect thinks he has no problem; that everything is running smoothly. However, in reality, this might not be the case. The customer might just be in some sort of denial phase or outright failed to see an underlying issue. By learning how to ask status quo questions, you're able to uncover any underlying issues your prospects might have. These new uncovered underlying issues is another opportunity to help them solve their problems, thus increasing your chances to make a sale.

As you may have already understood by this time, selling is asking first, then telling later. Surely, you've encountered annoying sales people in the mall where they keep rambling about the products features without asking the customer if they have a need for those features. Do not be like that.

PRINCIPLE 25

LEARN TO READ NON-VERBAL CUES FROM YOUR PROSPECT

Communication can be a tricky thing. You may be trying to communicate one message, but your prospect hears something entirely different; you may say one thing, but means something else. It reminds us of a classic scenario when a husband comes in and gets the cold shoulder. In bewilderment he asks his wife, "Honey, what's wrong?" She replies with an expressionless, "Nothing." And kudos the man who takes her word for it. She doesn't mean nothing by any stretch of the imagination.

The same crossed wires can happen with our prospects if we're not paying attention. When you're ready to present your sales presentation to the prospect, pay close attention to what they are not saying. In other words, they may be verbally saying, "Yes. you may proceed," but non-verbally, they're showing resistance. This may be when the prospect takes a step backwards, or sighs, or allows other people in the office to continually interrupt your presentation, or even checks their email. All of these are signs that the prospect is not bought in to your presentation. You can continue to make the presentation to this disinterested audience and waste time for both of you, or you can deal with it. As soon as you see one of those negative non-verbal messages, state the obvious without accusing the prospect of resisting. Don't attempt to present a solution to the prospect if they're giving you signals that he's still not ready to hear what you have as a solution. He will give you clues that his balance is not upset, or that he feels like he doesn't know enough about you or your solutions. Be careful. If you rush into the presentation before you build value and gotten another prospect, you'll come across as a pushy sales person. To identify the prospect's resistance, ask questions like:

- "It looks like you still have some reservations about hearing my presentation. Where are you uncomfortable?"

- "We understand that you're ready to consider a change. Did we misjudge the situation?"

- "What have you seen or heard that you don't agree with?"

At this point, you can answer any concerns or address any issues and then continue on with your presentation. Always be looking for the non-verbal body language that gives you signs of resistance, such as looking away, or handling their notes. And try to manage the situation.

Also, look for signs of encouragement. When the prospect leans forward, touches your product, smiles, nods or even rubs their chin are all non-verbal signs of showing interest in what you're saying. During your presentation, prospects are deciding whether your product will meet their needs at a price they're willing to pay. You must be able to read whether your information is leading them to say yes, no, or maybe. To successfully become an expert at reading your prospect's non-verbal cues, observe carefully the body language of each prospect that you see. And afterwards. record specific positive and negative body language responses. This will help you focus on this aspect of communication and keep you alert to all the signals your prospect is giving you.

> "IN ADDITION TO KNOWING YOURSELF, YOU MUST CONTINUE LEARNING ABOUT PEOPLE"

PRINCIPLE 26

AVOID OVERWHELMING THE PROSPECT WITH TOO MUCH INFORMATION

You are a professional sales person. We bet that you know your product so well that you could talk about it in your sleep. But this expertise can sometimes lead to problems. For example, have you ever found yourself putting your sales presentation on auto-pilot? You want to avoid this because it makes you seem like a robot and appear insincere and disinterested. Another problem that can arise is sometimes, when you are so familiar with your product, you assume the prospect is just as familiar. So you tend to hurry the presentation and close the sale too early. For example, notice some of your prospect knows about all the features of this car, just because they have driven other cars. Take the time to explain all the relevant features and benefits of your product or service, even though they may seem obvious to you. Your prospect will let you know if you are going too slowly, but they will not always let you know if you are going too fast.

On the other hand, one disadvantage of so much knowledge and enthusiastic confidence is that you probably believe the prospect wants and needs to hear every detail about your products. Remember, tone it down a notch and tell the customer or prospect about the relevant benefits and features. What prospects really want to hear is that you understand their needs and problems, and that there is a solution. When you introduce features and benefits in your presentation that are not relevant to the prospect's needs, you distract them with too much information. When you are asking questions to uncover their needs, you will begin to get a sense of what the problems are, what solutions you can offer, and what benefits are important to this particular prospect. Therefore, your presentation will be tailored to the prospect's needs; this prospects benefits and the solution this prospect has been looking for.

When you frame your presentation around this knowledge, you will not be as tempted to overwhelm them with every feature--only the ones which are relevant to this prospect. Now, after the sale has been made, it is okay to educate the prospect on more features or to bring up additional products that may solve other problems that the prospect may have.

The key point is that your presentation should always emphasize the product's features and benefits that have been uncovered during the question step of the sales process. Anything else is a distraction. To be able to tailor fit your presentation according to what your prospect really needs, you will want to listen and coach yourself to make sure you are not overloading your prospects and customers with too much information. Keep your sales presentation centered on a particular prospect's needs. We've mentioned that being enthusiastic about what you have to offer to the prospect is important. However, being overly enthusiastic can be detrimental to your sales efforts. They can be distracting and annoying. This of it as being in an online chat room, where flooding the chat box is considered annoying and rude.

PRINCIPLE 27

KNOW THE ADVANTAGES OF PRESENTING YOUR PRODUCT'S BENEFITS CLEARLY

Now, let's discuss how to present the benefits of what you sell clearly to your prospect. It's been observed that many sales people like to point out the features of their products, while in their minds they believe they are pointing out the benefits of what they are offering. Believe us when we say that there is a big difference.

First, let's get some definitions out of the way. A feature is a trait or characteristic of a product or service. In other words, what that product is. A function is the act the feature performs for the user. In other words, what it does. The benefit is what the feature does for the prospect. Let's go through these definitions together. Look at a ballpoint pen for example. The features we want to point out to you is the clip. But we're not going to spend time talking to you about the clip itself. We want to point out the functions of the clip. And that is it holds the pen in your shirt pocket. But we don't want to spend our precious time with you talking about the function of the clip. What you're interested in is what the clip does for you. The benefits to you are it saves you time by not misplacing the pen, you always know where to look for it, and it saves you money by not having to constantly replace the pen that you lost. Now, how do you say that conversationally? Well, it could sound like this:

"You said you're always losing you pen, which slows you down and waste money. One of the features of our pen is this clip. It's a strong

and more flexible clip than any other top selling pen. And it has been proven in a stress test. Now, the benefit to you is you always have your pen handy because it stays in your pocket. And you'll save money, because you won't be buying for your pens."

The most important step in that example--and more importantly for you--is to match your benefits with the prospect's needs. In a sales presentation, if you can show the prospect how he can receive all the benefits you described, does he care what you call it? Of course not. While we get excited about brand names, model numbers and other marketing identifications, most of the time a prospect doesn't care as long as it delivers the benefit. Be careful with overloading the prospect's head with information he doesn't need. Be sure they clearly understands what the product will do for them. To apply this information today, answer these questions:

1. What are the three most important parts, or aspects, or features of your product or service?

2. What advantage does that part or aspect perform? In other words, what does your product or service do?

3. What are the primary reasons that others would want to purchase your product or service? In other words, what benfits does your product or service do for the prospect?

One of the great ways I remind myself of this is to remember the acronym F.A.B. B. (Features, Advantages, Benefits). By answering these questions, you will have a list of features, advaqnatge, and benefits you can share with your prospects.

PRINCIPLE 28

BRIDGE THE FEATURE, FUNCTION, AND BENEFIT TO YOUR PROSPECT

Sales people need to clearly understand that prospects do not buy what the product is. They purchase the benefits that come about from the use of the product. For an average driver, Anti-lock braking systems or ABS may mean little or nothing at all until you point out that they help to avoid dangerous uncontrolled skidding by keeping the wheels from locking up. Steel belted radial might mean very little unless you explain that it enables the driver to get an extra 15000 safe miles out of a set of tires. Guaranteed renewable might mean little to a senior citizen, until you explain that the company can't cancel the policy at any age. Five inches of insulation mean nothing until you translate them into lower heating and air-conditioning cost. In short, all these people benefit when you describe a feature and function. To avoid confusion and appropriately make use of function, benefit and feature, we need to add the bridge. So what is a bridge? A bridge is basically something that you say to a customer or prospect that prepares them to hear the benefit of the product that you're about to pitch. The bridge phrase shouts, "Attention! Brace yourselves for the advantage, the benefit, and the main reason for you to purchase." Here are some examples of bridge statements:

- "The advantage to you Mr. Smith is.."

- "You will enjoy this because.."

- "The benefit to you is.."

So when you point out a feature and tell the prospect what it does to tie it down, you must personalize it with a benefit they would be interested in. For example, let's say we sell memberships to a gym. We might say:

" You stated that you prefer working out at night because it helps you relax. One of the features of our fitness centers is that it is open 24 hours a day. Since we never close, you can use the facilities any time. The advantage to you is you can work out and relax as late as you like."

You can probably understand why some people sell only functions. In other words, what it does. But beware of this trap. What your product or service may do is very interesting, and it may even convince a prospect that you know your business and understand the value of your product. However, functions probably won't cause the prospect to give you his or her money. That will happen when, and only when you persuade the prospect to take action by clearly spelling out what's in it for them. When you show the prospect the advantages they get from using the product or service, now you're both truly communicating. Paint a mental picture so your prospect sees your product's personal benefits. If you are struggling with the feature, function, or benefit for your product or service, imagine how your prospects must feel. If you don't clearly understand and can't clearly articulate the difference, you may be losing sales to those who can.

PRINCIPLE 29

LEARN TO LEAD WITH NEED

The previous lessons were about emphasizing the benefits of what you offer. But you want to be sure that you're not putting too much emphasis on your product to early. You want to lead with the need instead of leading with your product. For each product that you are presenting, state the need first and then link the need to the solution. In other words, your product and its features and benefits.

How can you lead with the prospect's needs if you don't know them? You can't. And that means before presenting your solution, you must be asking questions to find out the prospect's needs. You see, people do not buy products. They buy products of the product, or also known as benefits.

For example, we want a professional corporate image, not a suit. We want a good night's sleep, not necessarily a mattress. We want the bragging rights with our buddies, not a new golf club. Once we've established what the need is for the particular prospect, we will first state the need, use a transition question for the direct agreement, then present the product and its benefits as the solution. In other words, you must uncover the specific needs of the prospect that you can relate your product or service to.

Let's say we've been working with a prospect. We've used questions to find out that Wilson wants to have time to train a staff and more time to spend with his family. The barrier is his bad health. So we would say, "William, if we could show you a way that you could feel better, have time and energy to train your staff and participate in more activities with your family, would you be interested?"

You see, we lead with his most pressing need and then transition with a yes or no question, in which the obvious answer is, "Yes. I am interested." Now you have the prospect's attention. Then you go on to present your product or service with all its glorious benefits. Leading with a service or product's characteristics or features is meaningless. Why? Because that particular product feature you just stated may not be what the prospect actually needs. It's useless to go on and on about a product only to find out that the prospect doesn't have a need for it. This is what makes questions a crucial weapon for a sales professional. Without questions, you won't be able to uncover the need, which you can lead with when relating the benefits of your product or service.

To be successful in leading with the need, be conscious of how you transition to your sales presentation. After finding out the needs of your prospect, lead with the need and then tell the prospect the benefits of your solution. Make them realize, through benefits statements, that they indeed have a need for that particular service or product. It's not enough that you realize their need. They must also realize that they indeed have a need.

PRINCIPLE 30

LEARN HOW TO PAINT WORD PICTURES

Now, let's talk about the power that you have in the words you use. You want to be careful about the language you use. You need to use words that sell like, understand, proven, easy, proud, profit, and value. Some words, of course, will turn a prospect off; they "un-sell." The words deal, costs, pay, try, difficult, and obligation are things most prospects don't want to hear. They are more interested in hearing the word invest, instead of buy. We find it easier to make "deposits" each month than make "payments." Get rid of using words like we, I, us, me, in your presentation and replace it with the word "You & Your" followed by some benefits. Example is "Our customer service provides great service." instead say "You will love the customer service because they are attentive to your needs." Words that sell are very important. Here is another example, we use word pictures as a very positive approach to open the prospect's mind. Paint word pictures as often as you can. Here's one of our favorites:

There was once a housewife from New Jersey who wanted to sell her six-bedroom home since space is becoming an issue. She put the care of her house on the hands of three brokers, who in three months still cannot manage to sell the house. The housewife, with her uncanny sense of excellent advertising copy, managed to sell the house in one day. So you might be asking, how did she do it? Well, for starters, the brokers only ran typical, run-of-the-mill ads such as, "Home with an excellent fireplace, big garage, tile bath and hot water," or "House that is accessible to campuses, golf courses, supermarkets, primary schools, and golf courses." These ads did indeed stated facts. However, prospects do not buy facts or even benefits and features unless they can translate it to their own use. After the three months has passed, the housewife decided to run an ad of her own which says a little something like this:

"An extreamly nice home that will be missed. This home has made the family very happy. So many great memories have been created within its four corners. Unfortunately, the two bedrooms aren't enough for the growing family anymore, so time to move on. If you like to be cozy in front of the fireplace during cold seasons, or admire the beautiful woods during autumn through large windows, or maybe have a relaxing yard to rest during the summer seasons, or have an environment tranquil enough to hear the frogs croak and the birds chirp during spring and still have the city-like conveniences and utilities, then you will definitely love to purchase our lovely home. We surely don't want this nice home to be alone this coming Christmas."

The housewife received six responses from the ad the next day. And one of them was convinced enough to buy the home. As you can see, this technique of painting word pictures is not only easy, but it can also work for you. To learn to paint word pictures effectively, we encourage you to start painting those word pictures in your own mind. Share them with your friends and associates. Memorize them. Make certain you have them clearly in order, and then you will be able to use them effectively.

When you start painting those word pictures of satisfaction, gratifications, joy and delight with the prospect, you can see a benefit in using what you have to offer.

PRINCIPLE 31

LEARN TO URGE YOUR PROSPECT EMOTIONALLY TO TAKE ACTION TODAY

If a doctor just diagnosed you with a serious infection, would it not create a sense of urgency for you to take immediate action? Take the medicine before it gets worse. If you're a mechanic that just found a crack in your engine, would he not create a sense of urgency for you to get it fixed before the car breaks down and leave you stranded? If a plumber found a leaky pipe under your house, wouldn't you expect him to create a sense of urgency? Repair it before it develops any foundational problems? Each of these professionals uncovered a serious need and recommended an immediate solution. What would you think about a professional sales person who's not aggressively concerned about the customer to recommend purchasing one, or maybe even two of the products that would meet the need, fix the problem, or increase the satisfaction or gratification of the prospect sooner rather than later.

We know that in all presentations, we must lead with need. Emphasize benefits that are specific to the prospect. And pay attention to the prospect's non-verbal messages. To increase your closing ratio, you must also communicate a sense of urgency so the prospect will take action now. It's one thing to persuade the prospect that our products are the best, and another thing to persuade him to purchase now. The best way to create a sense of urgency is to paint a vivid picture of what the prospect would gain if he takes action now, and what he will lose if he waits.

These gains and losses must appeal to his emotions. Emotions moves us to action faster than logic will.

Can you think of an example of when this was true for you? Take for instance someone on a diet. Logically, the dieter knows to ignore the dessert at the end of the salad bar. But if the dieter emotionally needs that dessert, logic will not stop him. No matter how strong the facts are about the calories and fat included in that dessert, the dieter helps himself to a dessert to feed an emotional need. To get your prospect emotionally involved, he must be able to visualize the risk he is taking by not having the product; and experience the emotion of fear about that risk. The mind works in pictures. Words and stories paint pictures--both positive and negative.

To be able to urge your prospect emotionally to take action today, create some vivid word pictures to help the prospect picture how tragic it would be to go another day without the benefits of your product or service. Think about how you can describe what would happen if they fail to act now. Create a sense of urgency to make the buying decision today. Show them the cost they have to pay if they don't take advantage of what you're offering today. Show them the problems they might encounter if they don't get a particular service that you offer. Make them see different possibilities that might take place if they don't push through with the sale.

PRINCIPLE 32

MIND YOUR BODY LANGUAGE, CREATE A GOOD IMPRESSION

When you meet a prospect for the first time, they instantly--some say within 3-4 seconds--form an impression of you. Then you spend the rest of your time with that person either changing their mind or confirming what they thought. If you meet with your customers in person, one of the first things that people will notice about you is your appearance. The clothes you choose to wear make a statement about you.

We have a choice on what statement we want to make. Think about the people you will be presenting to. You always want to dress either at the level of dress they will have or higher, never lower. The statement you're striving for is, "We are like you. You can trust us." So when you're meeting with a group of corporate executives, you will probably want to wear your most professional clothes; a coat and tie.

If you're meeting with a technical staff, you might go with a casual shirt and pants. If you're meeting with a production line going over how the new equipment works, you'll probably want to dress in short sleeves and khakis. You get the point. Dress to make the statement that says, "You can trust us."

If you're meeting the prospect or customer face to face, there are several elements that come into play. Research indicates that when we communicate with someone face-to-face, only 7% of what they pick up on is our word choice, 38% is our tone of voice, and the biggest component is our body language, which is 55% of our message. In that light, we need to be careful with what our body might be saying, in contrast with what our words are saying. How you shake hands, stand, or sit during your presentation can speak volumes. And if you're not aware of it, you may be sending the wrong message.

You want to sit or stand in a neutral stance. Standing a certain way or sitting with your hands on the table a certain way don't say anything really. That means that the listener is not distracted by your body language and can focus on your message. Standing in a fig leaf can say different things to different people; closed off, nervous, stiff. We've asked a lot of people. And while we don't always get the same answer, we always get a negative answer. Standing with your arms crossed may be comfortable. But does it send the message you want? How does it look? Part of your message will probably say you're glad, but 55% percent of your message says, "You scare me!"

It is okay to be nervous. It is not okay to show nervousness. If you're on the phone, you take away 55% of how we communicate. Your body language, in this instance, your word choice and tone of voice become more important. To be able to create a good impression to your prospects or customers, look at yourself. What statement are you making? Is there something you need to change in your appearance to make the appropriate statement? Next time you're making a sales presentation, think about your body language. Are you being neutral, or is your body language saying that you want to be anywhere but with your prospect? These are subtle, yet important aspects to being a more professional sales person.

PRINCIPLE 33

LEARN HOW TO TAP INTO YOUR PROSPECT OR CUSTOMER'S EMOTIONS

When speaking with someone with the intent to persuade them, you need to have all the logical facts and reasons it's a good idea to take action. However, you must also tap into the emotional side to make your prospect want to take action. As we have pointed out in the previous chapters, people buy for emotional reasons and back it up with logical reasons. There are many ways to tap into people's emotions during your sales presentation. You can paint word pictures with vivid word choices. You can paint a pictures of the risk of not having the benefits of what you're offering. And you can also paint pictures with your gestures.

Gestures are simply an extended expression of you. Basically, it is hand and arm movements that make a point. This will help the audience follow what you're saying. It helps your audience stay with you; keep up with you during your presentation. We tend to think and store information in pictures rather than words. So the more you can help your prospect picture your message, the easier they will remember and be involved with your message. You may be thinking that you've always been told to stop using your hands. Actually, what they mean is to make your hand movements meaningful. In other words, make your hand movements specific and dovetailed with the words you're saying. Make a conscious effort not to make repetitive gestures. Repetitive movement is not using your hands effectively. It is annoying, distracting, and will most likely make your prospect disinterested in what you have to say.

However, matching a specific word with a specific gesture will make you more interesting as a presenter. And will help your customer or prospect paint a mental picture of what you're saying. For example, if you were selling software, then during your presentation you could say, "After working with our software overtime, it will begin to be intuitive to your needs and even perform multi-step processes for you with the click of a mouse." The mouse clicking or keyboard typing gestures add the needed polish to your presentation and impact to your words. To apply this technique effectively, look for opportunities in your presentation that lend themselves to gestures. Things like numbers, directions, and verbs are easy places to begin using gestures. This skill is a subtle skill to make your presentation even more interesting and professional. Make your gestures subtle and not overly profound. When talking about a storm or a specific weather event, don't wave your hands in the air like George from the jungle. It looks annoying, distracting, and unprofessional. Make your gestures minimalistic but still in tune with what you're saying.

Hone your gesturing skills by practicing in front of the mirror for at least 30 minutes every day and see how you look like. If your gestures look awkward and annoying, it is likely that the prospect will see it the same way as well. Practice is key to integrating gestures efficiently in any sales presentation.

PRINCIPLE 34

MAINTAIN EYE CONTACT THE CORRECT WAY WITH YOUR PROSPECT

You know that you can't trust a person who can't look you in the eye. While that may have some truth to it, the fact is the best con artist in the world can look you straight in the eye and take all your money. Even so, we still tend to associate good steady contact with your eyes to trustworthiness. Your prospects would buy from you for a number of reasons. And one of those reasons is because they trust you.

When presenting your solution to their problem, in other words during your sales presentation, it is important to practice good, steady eye contact. You can think of eye contact as a handshake. A weak handshake gives people a negative impression. A firm handshake gives people a positive impression. The same is true for your eye contact. Eye contact that is strong is called "eye clasp." This is when you make solid eye contact with another person for three, four, or five seconds. Now, most of us are comfortable looking at someone and then immediately looking away. But staying with the person--the prospect--for a full four seconds communicates trust, understanding, confidence, professionalism, and a whole host of other positive qualities.

Now, we don't expect someone to think about what they're saying and count at the same time. In other words, the prospect is going to be looking at you and you're going to be looking at them, you're not going to be counting one, two, three, four. Instead, to accomplish this three, four, or five seconds, just try to complete a thought or a sentence with someone before shifting your eye contact. Now on the other hand, don't stare. Going over five seconds can make the other person uncomfortable. If you're presenting to a group of people, spread the eye contact around to everyone. If you're presenting to just one, you want look at the prospect for 3-4 seconds and then shift your gaze to somewhere else. On the other hand, you want to make sure that you look at one or two people before you break eye contact when presenting to several people. Look at your notes or at your Power point presentation.

You want to avoid shifting your eyes back and forth between two or more people. This makes you look shifty-eyed and therefore not trustworthy. For some, this is what they call "crazy eyes." Be careful not to do this. Also, do not drop your eyes when you are handling an objection or going over the less desirable aspects of your product or service. Again, keeping steady eye contact will convey confidence, and competency on your part and in what you're saying. To effectively implement this skill today, Practice making three, four, or five seconds making eye contact with every person you have a conversation with today. Now you may feel uncomfortable at first, but your comfort level will grow as you practice more. As what we've mentioned before, practice makes perfect. Besides, you are more concerned at being effective than being comfortable, aren't you?

PRINCIPLE 35

LEARN HOW TO DEVELOP A 'CLOSING' ATTITUDE

If you want to be a successful sales person, you must develop a "closing" attitude. Another name for closing could be "need satisfaction." It's what you have been building up to do. You offer your product or service as they need solution. Closing sales don't have to be painful for you or the prospect. In fact, it's a win-win situation if you've done everything for the benefit of the prospect. Asking for the order is the natural progression that must occur. In sales, not asking for the sale is like running to the half-way mark of a marathon and then quitting. If you've already sourced a prospect, developed rapport, established trust, uncovered the need, and presented your product, why not go all the way and ask for the sale? By not asking for the sale, you've wasted your time and effort in laying the groundwork for the whole sales call. Asking for the sale is the final stage of any sales presentation.

Do it pleasantly. Do it professionally, and ask. The proper approach in following these suggestions will put you in a win-win situation. This means that you have now reached an agreement with the prospect and you clearly understand that the sales process is something you do for a person and not to that person. The closing attitude is your understanding that you are there to solve a problem or prevent some in the future. Not closing the sale will also give the prospect an impression that you're not sincere in helping them solve their problem. You just went there, told them what they wanted to hear, and then stepped away as if you've changed your mind. Not asking for the sale is considered taboo in the world of sales. Why in the world would go into the selling business if you have no intention of asking for the sale--selling--in the first place?

To develop a closing attitude, realize that regardless of the circumstances, technical knowledge, experience, investment, or anything else, always ask for the order. Don't be afraid, or even be ashamed, to ask for the sale. If your prospect says no, the reason is most often that they do not know enough to say yes. In that case, you begin the process of managing objections.

How do you effectively manage objections? You go and ask the prospect questions. In addition, you can also present them with new evidence and information in order for them to make a new buying decision. Go out there with a positive attitude and make those sales. Keep your enthusiasm up at all times. There may come a time when you would feel down about losing a prospect or a customer. Don't let disappointments pull you down. Shrug the disappointment off and proceed with the next prospect on the list. Do not waste your time dwelling on failures. Instead keep moving and focus on the next sale. Keep the mistakes that you've made in the past, if there are any, and then make sure you don't commit them on the next sales call that you make. Remember, nothing happens until somebody sells something. Let that person be you.

PRINCIPLE 36

LEARN TO MAKE USE OF TRIAL CLOSES

A trial close is a closing effort made in the sales process at an earlier time. It is commonly used to succeed interest or intent to close after a buying signal has been given by the prospect. Any time you ask a question to seek agreement on a minor decision that leads to the major decision. You're using a trial close, aren't you? These questions tell you if you're getting a "buy" from the prospect based on their response, don't they?

When you add a trial close, you are asking for action; a decision that leads to the sale. They can sometimes be referred to as direct agreement questions. This is not an attempt to close. But more a test to see if the prospect is getting closer to closing the sale. Some trial close examples are:

1. "Does that sound about right to you?"

2. "Along with that helmet, do these other safety items make sense together?"

3. "You don't want to delay in getting that compound interest, do you?

4. "It seems that you absolutely like this, is that true?"

Remember, you can't make anyone change his or her mind. You can only provide them new information to make a new decision. Each time you present new information, or benefit, ask a trial close question with it. For example, "Did we mention that the software is MAC compliant? Could your entire team benefit from the same upgrades?" or "This vitamin comes in liquid form, which means it enters your bloodstream faster than a solid tablet. This would go down easier and better, wouldn't it?"

Your trial closes could also start with "if." For example, "If this was only available with a fax machine model, it would still be a good deal, wouldn't it?" When you ask the question, pause. Let there be silence. You are watching and listening for your prospect's response. Observation is key in this instance. Was it a courteous "I guess so?" That means you've got more selling to do. Was it an enthusiastic "Yes?!" Maybe you've sold enough and it's time to ask for the order. Was it a skeptical or sarcastic answer? Then you've got to work towards adding value to your offer. Any of these signs is okay. It shows you where you are and how much further you have to go. Be careful about using a trail close too early in the process, or too often. You can annoy and even turn your prospects off. Use your good judgment and tune in to their body language and tone of voice to make sure there is no hint of annoyance.

You can implement the trial close technique today by practicing this concept on your friends or co-workers until they ask you to go away. Only with practice will this become natural for you. The right tone of voice with the right sincerity would let you and your prospect win. Trial closes is a way to tread the waters and see if the prospect is ripe for the pickings or not.

PRINCIPLE 37

LEARN THE THREE TESTED AND RELIABLE 'ASKING FOR THE ORDER' CLOSES

Although there are literally hundreds of ways to ask for the order, we will be sharing a few from the field that are tested and reliable. It is good if you know lots of different closes. But do you know them well enough to use them at a moment's notice in the proper sales environment? In other words, learn and practice many different kinds of closes. However, make sure you know them well and can use them for the genuine good of the prospect. The key is this: don't reinvent the wheel. Educate yourself on other people's experiences. After working with these closes a while, you will be able to personalize them and make them fit your sales presentation. The first close is the "Three questions" close. You use these three simple questions:

1. "Can you see where this would..?" and you insert the primary benefit that would cause the prospect to buy.

2. "Are you interested in..?" then you state the benefit again.

3. "If you were ever going to start this benefit, when do you think would be the best time to start?"

If you have made your presentation in such a way that you can expect an affirmative answer to the first question, then the process would work for you. It helps you tie the emotion of the decision to the logic of the decision. In the second question, what you may want to try is the probability close. Once your prospect is at the moment of truth, you may ask a follow-up question to obtain the order or the information you need to get the order. Remember to choose your words carefully. You don't want to plant seeds of disinterest or the impression of falling for anything. Wait patiently for the response. This close is best used when you are very close to getting the order, but feel there's some resistance you need to get into the open. Handling this resistance or objection gets the problem into the open and enables you to deal with each one properly.

Finally, the summary close is a good basic close to know and use. Even though it may seem very basic to you, don't minimize the significance of what may seem obvious. In the summary close, you recap the areas of the presentation that caused the light bulb on your prospect's head to light up, and then ask for your order. After you receive a favorable reply, you definitely should go for the close and say, "..then let's get the order started." You see, during the sales process, the prospect gets excited about certain benefits you can provide. But during the sales process, that excitement may begin to die down due to any number of circumstances or directions.

By summarizing, you rekindle the flame at the moment you're asking the prospects to make their investment. The more "feeling" they have at this moment, the more sales you will close. To successfully implement this technique in your sales process, take each of these three closes and work on making it fit your personality, your product, or service, and then practice, practice, practice. You will be sure to close more sales more often with practiced closes that you can deliver with confidence and ease.

PRINCIPLE 38

LEARN THE 4 REFINED 'PERSUADE THE PROSPECT TO AGREE AND BUY' CLOSES

Perhaps the most frustrating experience a sales person has is to gain agreement from the customer. Yes, the product is good, it will save money, he does need it, he would like to have it, he really could afford the payment, but no, he is not going to buy. Many times this indicates that the prospect has been convinced of the merits--or at least appears to be convinced and sold. But he has not been persuaded to take action. At this point in the sales process, it becomes necessary for you to know different closing methods in which to help persuade your prospect to agree to your solution. Right now, we'll share with you four more closes that have been refined out in the field and brought to you for your success.

1. One of the easiest closes to incorporate into your sales presentation is the "alternate of choice" close. Never give the prospect a choice between something and nothing. Let him choose between something and something else. This close can be used under many circumstances. It may sound like, "Shall I ask the company to ship it as soon as possible, or would two weeks be better?" or "Would you like me to rotate the tires too, or just do the oil change?" or "Do you want our store to hem your slacks, or will you take them to your tailor?"

2. The previous purchase close is another good close to learn. The best way to get a prospect to make a favorable new decision is to make him happy with an old decision. Complement his past purchases with specific reasons why they were smart. For example, good quality, or they used a company with a good reputation. If you attack the previous purchases the prospect has made, then you are attacking them personally. And this does not build rapport.

3. You may be able to use the "spare" close. If you have a product that wears out and needs to be replaced, this close may work for you. When you are conducting a service call, and you find a part that is wearing out, ask the customer to give you the spare part and you will replace it free of charge, since you're already there.

   Nine times out of ten the customer will not need or have a spare part. Express your genuine concern for their safety or their convenience and offer them a replacement part. When they say yes, bring two parts; one to replace, and one to keep as a spare. Many times the customer will purchase both.

4. If you have many items on sale, the accessory close may be perfect for you. After your customer has made the initial major purchase, schedule a service call with them. Before you go, prepare a supplementary order that works well with the initial major purchase. When you get there and you have completed your service, present the supplementary order. After looking at the order and seeing

how well it works with the first purchase. Many prospects will become enthusiastic buyers of the supplementary order.

> "EVERY SALE HAS FIVE BASIC OBSTACLES: NO NEED, NO MONEY, NO HURRY, NO DESIRE, NO TRUST"
> ZIG ZIGLAR

PRINCIPLE 39

LEARN TO TRY MORE THAN FIVE TIMES TO ASK FOR THE ORDER

So, what keeps you from closing? Research from Dr. Herbert Williams of Harvard discloses that 46% of the sales people he interviewed asked for the order once, and then gave up. 24% asked for the order twice before quitting. 14% asked the third time. And 12% held in there to make several attempts before throwing in the proverbial towel. That is 96% who left after four attempts. However, similar research shows that 60% of sales are made after a fifth closing effort.

How many times do you attempt to close the sale before you leave? If the answer isn't five, then you may need to go back and try again. For those of you who are reluctant to ask for the order more than once or twice for fear of coming across as high-pressure sales people, think about this: When baseball pitchers reject the ball, the ball is returned to the umpire who puts it in his pouch with the other baseballs. Later, that same ball would be given to the pitcher. Seldom, if ever, is the same ball rejected twice. In the same way, the prospect will look at your offer in a different light; the second, third, forth, and even the fifth time. Just as a professional baseball umpire offers the same baseball to the pitcher, so must the professional sales person offer the same product to the prospect several times. Asking your prospect for the order more than four times can be exceptionally tough if you:

    a.) don't believe in the service or product that you sell

b.) didn't go through the initial sales process steps properly

c.) don't even expect to make the sale at all

Not so incidentally, note that between each closing effort, you must give additional reasons, features, functions, and benefits for the prospect to make the "Yes" decision today. When you offer added information, you allow the prospect to make a new decision based on additional information.

Many times we don't ask the question because we don't want to hear the "No." This is where you'll want to give yourself a gut check. To do this, you need to debrief each sales call immediately after the presentation. That is, get alone and relive the experience. This is most effective when you keep a written journal of your observations. Ask yourself, "Did I ask for the order? If not, why?" If some of your answers are, "...the timing just wasn't right," "The prospect was distracted," "...there were too many people around," or "...she needed to take a breather and think things through," realize these are often excuses for not asking for the order. Don't misunderstand.

There are occasions when it's wise to back away and return another day, especially if the amount of investment you're asking the prospect to make is significant. However, in an overwhelming majority of the cases, you need to be honest with yourself and admit you're just making excuses for yourself and you need to ask for the order. To learn how to ask for the order every time, count how many times you asked for the order with each prospect today. If it's less than five, then tomorrow, commit to yourself that you'll just try one more time with each prospect.

PRINCIPLE 40

MAINTAIN A RELATIONSHIP WITH THE CUSTOMER AFTER THE SALE

After you have successfully closed the sale and have the cheque in hand, now what? Many sales people think this is the end of the sales process, unless they tell you they needed to sell to that customer some more. A professional sales person realizes that the close is just the beginning of a long-term relationship. Your interest in the customer after the sale plays a major role in whether he or she will help you make additional sales.

You started the relationship based on trust. And for the relationship to continue, the trust must continue to grow. Customers must be managed reliably and confidently. You probably have many opportunities to contact the customer immediately after the sale is finished. A handwritten thank you note will certainly make you stand out from a crowd of vendors. The same can be said with a follow-up phone call after product installation. Do they require a product training? A personal invitation to a webinar, teleconference, or in-office demonstration would continue to foster the relationship. It's not necessary for you to be the person doing the training or even for you to attend. Your role is to integrate the customer into your organization's processes as seamlessly and painlessly as possible--for the customer.

What happens when a customer service issue pops up? Are you quick to forward that email or angry voice mail to the "customer service department?" After all, it's their job. But wait, you have some responsibility in the process. Whether it's a quick introduction to the person or department that will be resolving the issue, or a phone call to make sure the issue was resolved to the customer's satisfaction, the point is they have a relationship with you first, and your company second. Help them navigate through a customer service issue. What are some opportunities you have throughout the year to contact your customers? Well, for starters, you may have product updates, or when delivering company news. Making a "checking in" call would also be appreciated. But squeezing this into your already busy week is probably the biggest issue or excuse you have. However, the benefits of maintaining strong relationships with your customers outweigh the hassle of fitting them into your schedule.

Depending on your situation, you can take the early part of the morning, or the late part of the afternoon and spend 15 minutes each day in customer service. To maintain a good sales person-customer relationship after the sale, make an appointment with yourself everyday this week to spend 15 minutes daily writing notes, making phone calls, or checking in with customers who already purchased from you. They will appreciate the attention and reward you with future sales and referrals. The customer will feel that although the sale has been finalized, you still have their welfare in mind; that you're still there to help them when a problem arises. If you're lucky, not only will you develop a long lasting sales relationship, but also a personal friendship. Being friends with a customer means that you now have an inexhaustible source of business.

PRINCIPLE 41

LEARN TO ASK FOR REFERRALS

At the end of the sales presentation, whether it results in a "yes," "no," or "maybe," the successful sales professional always asks the prospect for the names of people who might benefit from using the product or service just described. You really have to ask yourself about your level of belief in what you're selling if you're not willing to ask this question.

Referrals keep the sales professional in business. Remember, no matter how good your product may be, or regardless of the quality of your presentation, you are bankrupt and out of business if you don't have someone to tell your story to. Customers tend to refer you to people on similar social or business levels as themselves.

If you have a customer who fits your profile of a good customer, meaning he has a need for your product and a way to pay for your product, it is more than likely that his social and business associates will be very much like him. If you didn't ask the customer the close of the sale, you can always go back and ask later. When asking satisfied customers for referrals, you must first make sure they are in fact satisfied. Clear up any service, billing, or product problems they tell you about. Even if you can't fix it yourself, alert the company and follow-up after the company has corrected it. Then, ask your prospect if he or she is pleased enough with your service to refer you. You can say something like:

"Fred, it would be a privilege to help your friends and business partners the same way I'm helping you. If you would be comfortable enough to share their names and information with me, I guarantee I will do my best to treat them the same way I'm treating you, or would you rather call them yourself and introduce me."

Start by asking for names, then go back and ask for information about each one. Sometimes, it helps to jog the customer's memory by painting a picture of where that friend is. For example, at the office, the club, the board of directors, or the neighborhood. Once you have the names, ask your customer whom to call on first and how to prioritize the other names. The key to continue to get referrals is to report back to your customer and let him or her know the results of your calls. Let them know whether it was good, bad, or pending. With that kind of professionalism, they are likely to think of more referrals to give you. Again, before you go asking for referrals, make sure you clear up any pending problems with the service, the product, or the company. No prospect in their right mind would want to refer a company or sales person that they are dissatisfied with.

To learn how to ask for referrals effectively today, ask one of your customers for a referral. Once you see how easy it is, this may become your best lead source.

PRINCIPLE 42

DEVELOP VOICE INFLECTION AND VOICE MODULATION

Accarding to Zig Ziglar, "If you're going to build your sales career to the fullest, you've got to do something that 95% of all sales people never do. They never deliberately train themselves on how to use their voices more effectively." They don't do any work toward developing voice inflection and voice modulation. The very first thing we would recommend you to do is record your sales presentation. Start recording from the beginning of the conversation all the way through how you manage objections and to close the sale. Then listen several times to what you have said and the way you have said it.

You're going to be amazed to discover that your effectiveness, not withstanding most of what you say, is superfluous. In other words, you talk too much and you often speak in a monotone. You will be shocked at the non-answers you give to questions, objections, and the number of times you heard what the prospect said but missed what he was saying. When you listen back to your presentation, ask yourself whether you yourself would buy from that person you just heard. We will give you just one example of how you can use your voice effectively in a sales presentation. Although we must point out that your voice is critical in all parts of the presentation.

Here we're talking about a close; when you have asked for the order and you get a price question. We're sure that every sales person reading this book has one time or another encountered a price objection. When your prospect or customer says, "The cost is extremely lucrative," or "That is more than what we're prepared to pay," you can repeat almost verbatim what the prospect said then make your voice inflection up high so that it sounds like a question. The voice inflection is important here because you're creating a situation that forces the prospect to defend his or her statement instead of you justifying the cost. There's quite a difference. One puts you on the defense, and the other puts you on the offense. The difference is substantial. Instead of you trying to defend yourself against his objection, you must raise your voice inflection, return the objection to the prospect in a "questioning" manner, and then make him defend his own objection. This is a simple technique, but is not easy.

It will help you to clearly understand the prospect's objections. Is it really price, or is it something else? To be able to effectively use your voice inflection and modulation to your advantage today, we want to strongly encourage you to record your presentation and listen back to it. That would be one of the most critical things that you can do to help yourself move to the next level of success in your sales career. Practicing sentences with different emphasis on different words will help you train your voice to have more inflection. This will make you more interesting to listen to and will help you to communicate more effectively.

PRINCIPLE 43

LEARN TO LOVE QUESTIONS AND OBJECTIONS

Objections are the key to closing a sale. The person who sells exotic animals get three commonly asked questions: Where does it go to sleep? What kind of food does it eat? and who cleans up the wastes it leaves behind? Now, you may not be in the business of selling elephants, but all sales professionals' deal with objections and questions.

Many sales people fear that these objections and questions steer the prospect towards the dreaded "No" response when making an attempt to finalize and close the sale. However, objections are the sales person's best buddy. A question or an objection indicates interest or feeling; an uncompleted desire for your product or service. Think about it. Try to think of something that doesn't pique your interest whatsoever. Whether you thought of basketball, opera, fishing, golf, tennis, ballet, race car driving, you probably have no questions or objections because you have no interest. Real selling experts anticipate questions and objections for the reason that not many sales are made or orders placed without a prospective client display enough interest to raise objections and ask questions.

Now that you're convinced that it is good for the prospects to ask questions and raise objections, what happens when your answers are not satisfactory and the prospect says no? Once your prospect has said no, they're not going to change their minds and buy from you. Now you may be thinking that we're crazy; that you've had plenty of prospects say no once, only further into the conversation to say yes to your offer. That's because your prospects will make a new decision based on additional information. You see, when prospects say no, the successful sales professional understands that "no" must mean the prospects don't know enough to make the right decision. Never argue with the prospect. You'll always lose. You may win the argument, but you'll lose the relationship of a prospect or a long-time satisfied customer. Instead, just understand that you haven't finished your job. And accept responsibility for going back and providing the information asked.

With additional information, they will now know enough to make a favorable, and hopefully new, decision. Just like the analogy we've made prior about the baseball pitcher and the umpire, seldom will they reject the same offer twice. Why? Because each time you offer a product or service to the prospect, you will also be giving them new information where they will base their buying decision. To be able to effectively apply this technique in your sales process today, get excited when you hear objections. Know that you have an interested prospect in front of you. Work on providing additional information to them so that the prospect can make a new decision. Love questions and objections because it shows you certain areas of improvement with your product or service. Think of objections as areas where you can prove to the prospect that the service or product that you're selling is exactly what they need.

PRINCIPLE 44

LEARN THE RIGHT TIME TO HANDLE OBJECTIONS AND QUESTIONS EFFECTIVELY

When do most of your objections occur? If you received the same objection during all your presentations, then you probably need to review your presentation. Ask yourself if you're including information in the presentation that anticipates the objection and answers it before the prospect has a chance to voice it, or if one of the prospect's criteria that you uncovered when you were asking questions is something that you know you can deliver, you can bring it up yourself and be on the offense instead of the defense. Here's an example:

"Mr. Grimes, you said you only buy from companies who've been in business for more than ten years. You know we have a four year track record. But with all the experience in your group, we do have over 35 years of expertise."

Of course, dealing with the objection in the middle of your presentation is difficult, unless you are prepared. Always acknowledge that you heard it by briefly promising to address it in your presentation, or by stopping your presentation to test it to see if it's something that's really important to the prospect. You can test the validity of an objection by saying, *"Amanda, suppose that were not an issue. Then would you consider what we have to offer?"* You can also test an objection by asking, *"Is that the only thing that's holding you back from closing the sale?"*

Most often than not, prospects object when they hear or see

something they don't agree with. Usually, it comes after you've asked a trial close question. Handle the objection by using the process that we'll discuss in the next chapter. There are also times when you should not address the objection immediately. You could acknowledge it with a smile, or a quick pause. But delay your answer if you think the prospect is not completely serious about the objection.

Pay attention to his non-verbal language; their body language to help determine how serious his objection is. If he throws his hands up in the air while saying the price is too high, he is probably more serious than if he said it with a quick wink and a grin. Your timing in responding to him is in proportion to the seriousness of the objection. Here's a caution: If he brings it up a second time, it is important to him and you must handle it immediately. Handle it in a professional and courteous manner. Again, objections are not something to shy away from. They're a chance to further educate the prospect on the benefits that you're offering. To make use of this technique now, listen to how you handle objections. During presentations, record yourself and listen to them after. Are the same ones coming up repeatedly? Do you sound defensive when answering? Do you argue with the prospect? Coach yourself on how to address objections professionally and with confidence. Learn the proper timing in addressing the objection or question. This is crucial if you're looking to successfully close the sale.

PRINCIPLE 45

LEARN HOW TO MANAGE OBJECTIONS

Sales Objections. Don't you just hate them? Now, we're going to get serious about managing and overcoming sales objections. We're going to cover four specific principles, which are:

1. Whoever has the most information, has the most influence - Now what does that mean? The more information you have about the customer, the prospect or suspect, it's easier to ask questions, gather more information and overcome objections. You've got to do your homework. If you don't have enough information about the customer before the objection, it is going to be very difficult to manage and overcome that objection. Make sure you're always asking questions. You're only as good as your information. Whoever has the most information, has the most influence. Remember, information is power.

2. People will make new decisions only when given new information - Again, we can't stress this enough. If you haven't made a sale on a prospect, then go back to that prospect without anything new to tell him, he's going to make the same decision. Therefore, think about it today. What new evidence can you bring to this person that will allow him to make a new decision? People make new decisions if, and only if, they are presented with new information about the product or service.

3. Question the objection so that you can understand the objection and identify the objection - There are two things going on here. You must ask questions so that you can fully understand the objection, and identify if that's a true objection. You don't want to deal with false objections. Therefore, you must question the objection to determine if it's true or false.

4. You overcome objections with evidence; not lip service, not emotion, but factual beneficial evidence - You may have a third party story to tell this person for evidence. You may have a statistic. You may have a demonstration. If the product is where you can demonstrate it and actually have the person sit down and operate the product; drive the product that is evidence that may overcome objections.

Again, the four principles are as follows: First, you need information because if you have information, you have influence. Second, people do things for their reasons and not yours, which means people will make new decisions when you give them information for their reasons. Third, objections have to be questioned so that you can understand and identify the objections. Lastly, overcome objections by using evidence; facts, statistics, third-party stories. Never handle an objection with an opinion. Opinions are subjective and holds no weight against proven facts. Don't be afraid of objections. Welcome objections because they can be your friend. If you plug in to one of these four principles, you'll be more successful today. Handle enough objections so that you'll get used to it. You may also listen to more experienced sales professionals on how they manage their prospect or customer's objections. Learn from your colleagues experience just as you learn from your customer or prospect's experience.

"SELLING IS CHALLENGING.
IT DEMANDS THE UTMOST
OF YOUR CREATIVITY AND
INNOVATIVE THINKING"

PRINCIPLE 46

DO VALUE ADDED SELLING

You should know more about your customer than you do about your products. The more you know about your customers, the easier it is to communicate effectively with them. The more you know about your customers, the more solid your relationship is going to be with them. And the more you know about your customers, the easier it is for you to add value to your products and services. Now, we'll examine methods of adding value by your actions and by your concerns for your customers. Just what is added value? It is anything you do to serve your customers beyond their expectations. This may require you to think above and beyond your normal duties and responsibilities. Value-added is creating a pleasant surprise in the mind of the customer.

Now, value added selling is not dropping the price when the customer reacts negatively to the price tag. That is discount selling and we're not talking about discount selling. The trick to adding value is that the value is defined by the customer, not by you. Here's an example: You may have had a sales person tell you in the past that their package includes 24 hours of technical expertise that's available to you. Now, that is added value. But you may be willing to buy from a discounter and pay a per usage fee for that technical help. So the technical expertise at that package is not a value to you. This means that what is valuable to one customer may be perceived as not as valuable to another. Now, here's the big question. How then do you know how to exceed a customer's expectation? If you've been doing a professional job of selling up to this point, then you should know an awful lot about the customer.

By spending so much time at the beginning of the sales cycle asking questions and listening carefully, you have an idea of what is important to that customer. It may be speed. In that case, you highlight the quick turn-around time that your company is known for. It might be that you learn that their cash is tight. So you highlight your payment terms and how to schedule payments. Value added selling is important for several reasons. It allows you and your company to separate yourself from the competition. It creates a positive impression in the minds of your customer. It improves your word-of-mouth advertising and it creates an upbeat and positive environment at your place of business.

As it becomes more and more difficult to separate yourself from the competition, you need to understand that you are more into selling relationships. That's right. Selling relationships. You see, you're not in the selling business. You're in the people business. The more value you give people, the more willing they are to transact business with you. One of the best indicators of good customer service is the perception--by your customers--that you have exceed their expectations. Selling is not just a constant, competent job. It's exceeding customer's expectations time and time again

PRINCIPLE 47

LEARN TO UPSELL EVERY TIME

Upselling is a term used to describe moving a customer up to an upgraded product or adding a different product or service at an increased cost. Upselling is something that you do for the customer, not to the customer. In other words, it should provide an advantage or benefit to your customer. Upselling occurs after the customer has made the initial buying decision. You want to offer additional related products to their initial purchase. The classic example of upselling is when you place your order for a drink or burger in a fast-food store, and they always say, "Would you like fries with that?" How strange would it be if they asked, "Would you like car insurance with that?"

Educating the customer about other products or services that compliment their initial purchase is also one of upselling's main aim. Do you have volume discounts, extended warranties, protective storage bags for the product, or software? You get the idea. There are three basic methods you can use to upsell when dealing with a customer, either face-to-face or on the phone. First, you can ask a question. Second, make a suggestion. Lastly, explain the advantages. Let's look at the first method, which is asking a question. Questions will help you have a basis for offering the upsell. Ask how they plan on using the product or how often they will be using the product. For example:

"Mr. Sanchez, how many of these brochures do you think you will use in a month? You may be interested to know that we have volume discounts that may prove beneficial to you. Let me tell you what they

are and see if they make sense to you."

After asking a question, you may also make use of the second method, which is making a suggestion. If you know the buying trends of your customers and your products, you can say. *"Other people who have purchased this product have also shown interest in these products."*

Lastly, you can also make use of the third method and explain what the options are and the advantages. Many sales people leave money on the table because they didn't explain all the options to the customer. You can say, *"Mr. Wilson, here's an option. And let me explain the advantage to you."* For example, this may sound like, *"Mr. Wilson, you said that you have been travelling a lot lately. I'd like to explain the advantages of the nationwide membership program and how it will benefit you."*

You would then proceed to explain the benefits and ask if he is interested in enrolling in the program. So when should you upsell? There are opportunities all around the sales process. You can email existing customers offering a product they don't have, or that you think they may like based on what you know about them. You can also suggest a complimentary product they may want when you call to thank them for the order. Of course, during the buying phase of the sale, it is a good time to suggest additional purchases. These are up-sale and down-sale opportunities that will compliment and benefit the prospects original purchase

PRINCIPLE 48

LEARN THE PROPER TELEPHONE SKILLS

Previously we have discussed how to overcome call reluctance. Now, our focus will be making your business phone calls effective and professional. Telephone skills are not to be taken for granted. Like so many other things in life, there's nothing simple about the masterful use of the telephone as a business tool. At no time and at no other place are listening skills as important as when you were handling a business telephone call. When you're on the phone, you have nothing to go on except a person's voice and what they happen to be saying. With this in mind, it is extremely important that you go in to any business telephone conversation knowing the five basics of establishing a good telephone presence.

Telephone basic number one is Attitude. Here's a point that we've already made in other chapters, but it is so important that we'll make it again: Your attitude is paramount. You must project a winning, cooperative, can-do attitude at all times. The key to maintaining a positive attitude is maintaining the perception that every call is an opportunity, not an annoyance. You know you can hear "attitudes" over the phone. Your customer or prospects can tell if you are smiling, annoyed, or happy. Whatever attitude you have is clearly projected over the phone. So put a smile in your voice by putting a smile on your face.

Telephone basic number two is preparation. Have what you need before you begin making your prospecting calls. Have pens, pencils, paper, a resource material, computer, anything you're going to need immediately available. When you are making a call, understand your sales objective and leave nothing to chance. Know clearly what you're trying to achieve. Is it a face-to-face appointment to close a sale, or to gain permission to send more information? Whatever the objective, you need to have it clearly in your mind before you make the call. Making a call with a "let's see where it takes us" attitude will not consistently take you where you want to go.

Telephone basic number three is Getting Started. Whether you're placing or receiving a call, the first 10 to 15 seconds sets the tone for the entire conversation. If you have a spiel from which you do not digress, then even the most challenging phone calls will start off on the right foot and continue smoothly.

Telephone basic number four is to remember to keep it professional. This refers to the fact that as a professional sales person, you have to be capable of conveying a professional presence over the phone. You can't afford to answer the phone with a "proper and rehearsed" reply only to accidentally hang up on a customer or prospect when trying to transfer them or put them on hold. There are numerous common events that are likely to occur during the course of an average telephone call. Take the time to become proficient at them. We all know people who have worked in a given office situation for years and still don't have any idea of how to transfer or conference a call. Learn the system that you work with so that you give the customer the security of knowing they are dealing with a professional.

Telephone basic number five is Try not to repeat your self too many times. You could actually sell them on not buying from you because they feel you are being pushy and that you are only after the sale. If it is because you can't hear the person on the other line, offer to call them back. If the customer has an accent or is difficult to understand, be patient, offer to send them an email with the information.

Telephone basic number six is to be aware of your lasting impressions. The last thing the person on the other end hears will possibly be the only lasting impression you will leave. Leave a good impression. The end of any call should include a thank you.

"YOU GET PAID ACCORDING TO YOUR OWN EFFORTS, SKILL, AND KNOWLEDGE OF PEOPLE"

PRINCIPLE 49

LEARN TO USE THE VOICEMAIL AS A TOOL

I'm sure you will agree that technology has changed the face of business. People have come to expect instant solutions, instant information, and instant answers to their problems. You must be in constant communication with your customers and your prospects to gain and keep their attention. With all the different options available to a sales person and how you communicate with your customers and prospects, it should make your life easier. However, that is not necessarily the truth.

Now, we're going to discuss and focus on one specific technology: The voicemail. How can you use your voicemail to your advantage when you're prospecting. If you leave a message with just your contact information, you're probably frustrated because you get very few people calling you back. Instead, work on a professional, appealing voicemail that will pique someone's interest enough to get them to call you back right away. Here are a few guidelines as you compose your compelling voicemail:

1. It probably goes without saying that you need to keep it short; no longer than 20 seconds or they will delete your message.

2. Be unique. Do not leave a message that will blend in with the other ones that the prospect may have waiting when they return from a meeting. Have a standard mes-

sage that you use. But if you know anything about the company or the person you're calling, be sure to mention it so that you have built-in familiarity and create a connection. In the previous chapters, you were taught how to create general benefit statements. You may want to go through them again because this is the perfect place to use that statement.

3. Let your voice show your enthusiasm. You're doing them a huge favor by offering them your exceptional product or service, aren't you? Let your voice show that and share your enthusiasm. Also, clearly state your name, company name, phone number, and one or two benefits of your prodcut or services that may appeal to this prospect specifically. In addition, you may want to let them know what's in it for them. In other words, your general benefit statement. It might sound like this:

"Mr. Hobbs, my name is George Bracken from California Automation. We're calling to see if you might be interested in bringing your energy cost in under budget this year. We would like to schedule 15 minutes with you to show you some hard numbers for the amount of square footage you support. You can reach me at 555-3546. Again, that's 555-3546."

To be able to apply voicemail skills today, compose your general benefit statement and make a script for your voicemail messages. Try several different ways to deliver your statement until you find the one that's causing people to listen and call you back. This may take some perseverance or practice. But once you find a way to make your voicemail work for you, you will find it to be a great sales benefit for you. Try it on a friend and see if they call you back. You should also call yourself and try it on your own voicemail. Listen to it and see if it flows and sounds enticing enough for a callback.

"If you are not taking care of your customer, your competitor will"
Bob Hooey

PRINCIPLE 50

LEARN TO USE EMAIL EFFECTIVELY

Do you use email effectively in building your business? You may have tried and failed before, but listen closely to these tips and see if you can make your email work for you more successfully. You can use email to educate your customers about the products they have already purchased as well as what else they need that you offer. Keep in contact with your customers regularly; at least monthly and at the most weekly. It's important that every email you send to an existing customer contain information that they can use for their business in relation to what you offer. In other words, don't constantly send emails asking them just for more business. That will guarantee that your emails will go unread and eventually cause negative perceptions about you and your company. The good news about these kind of emails is that you invest time upfront creating them, but after you have developed them, they can be used over and over for any customer who's in that particular part of your product cycle.

If you want to use email as a prospecting tool, there are a few ideas to keep in mind. Of course, the first thing you must consider is whether your email list is appropriate. Do you have the correct list of people for your offering? Target your emails to the audience most likely to be in the decision making process for your offering, or your email will likely fall into cyberspace. Secondly, give the prospect a reason to buy from you. Offer a discount, a free upgrade, a premium service for a regular price, anything that motivates a person to respond to your offer. Be careful about giving a laundry list of products from which the prospect can choose. There's substantial evidence that a one product offering does better than a multiple product offering.

When creating the email, remember that just like voicemail, you have little time to capture the prospect's interest. You can even start the email with a benefit that will capture their attention and make them want to read more. Say something like, "How does saving 30% on your energy cost sound to you?" Then you could go on into detail about what you have to offer and how they can take advantage. Make sure your email is easy to read with absolutely no misspelled words or bad grammar.

Use of color is a good thing, unless there's too much of it. Try to look at your email as a prospect and ask yourself whether you would read it yourself. The last idea for email that you can use effectively when prospecting is the use of articles and newsletters. Your company may have a newsletter and a list of subscribers that can be used for email marketing. If so, that's a great advantage for you. If you're an independent sales person, or you don't have an organization that has an e-newsletter, you'll want to consider having one of your own list of clients and prospects. You can find an abundance of interesting articles on the internet that can be reprinted in your e-newsletter. And of course, any short articles that you write will certainly be appreciated for their expertise on your products or services. If you want people to open your emails and then actually read them, add value to them by adding a timely article.

ONE LAST MESSAGE

"We are what we repeatedly do. Excellence, therefore, is not an act but a habit" — Aristotle

If we're honest with ourselves, this quote will resonate within. We are most known by what we do, not what we say. If we are consistent in our actions and our work ethic, people take notice. Success is a measure of doing the common things uncommonly well. Don't do a good job, do a great job!

By following these principles, you should have no issues in increasing to your next level as a Sales Person and moving your way up in the success ladder. Consistently successful behavior translates to excellence. Truly successful people have integrity, a strong work ethic, they play full out, they have a desire to succeed and the tenacity to keep working and to keep learning even when things aren't going well. They don't give up easily; they keep moving forward, regardless of how many times they're knocked back.

I have been through some incredible life events. I have had great success and more than a few failures with my dreams and projects. The principles of sales in this book are the lessons that I have learned and adapted in my life to help me succeed. I believe that the true success is not achieving the end result but the journey to achieving that success. What you learn and who you become on the way is the true to success.

Two things I have learned on my way and I believe we can agree on, you miss all the shots you don't take and there is no traffic at the top of the freeway to greatness.

Make sure to always be honest with yourself. Work hard. Don't give up. Be consistent and persistent. Do a great job with everything you commit to and enter every commitment with success on your mind.

Don't wait for success to come to you. Be proactive to ensure that you attain the success you desire. Take the initiative to do more than is expected of you each day. Be excellent in your work. Then, when the opportunity presents itself, make the most of it. Ask yourself every day, "Am I consistent in my actions? Do I do my best work each and every day? Am I providing my commitment to excellence rather than mediocrity? Am I doing more than is expected?" If you can answer yes to all those questions, you are truly "Starting With YOU in Sales".

Remember, Don't ever stop investing into your continued education with personal development. You must always continue raising your personal development level so you can continue raising your success level. Never expect your success level to be at a 7 to 8 while your personal development level is at a level of 4 or 5.

I live by a motto and that is to always to inspire, motivate and empower others and by doing so I believe that success will manifest within my life. So I encourage that you do the same and that is to pay it forward by passing along a copy to your friends and family so you can help to make a positive difference in their lives and you too can manifest success within your life by blessing others.

Thank you again for reading this book. Make sure to read it a couple more times until these principles become second nature.

Mike Driggers

ABOUT THE AUTHOR

Mike Driggers Is a Top selling author, International in demand celebrity speaker, the world's leading Authority Marketing Agent, consultant, business owner and master strategist who inspires, motivates, and empowers people worldwide. Mike has been featured on ABC, NBC, FOX, CBS, PBS, USA Today, Business Journal, Wall Street Journal and the Brian Tracy Show. Mike is recognized as one of the world's most requested business, sales & marketing consultant. He is an in-demand international celebrity business and motivational keynote speaker who has delivered over 2500 presentations worldwide. Mike consistently wows audiences with his entertaining and interactive keynotes, seminars, workshops, coaching, and training programs.

Mike is the author of several books titled "Mastering of The Mind Set", "Unleash The Intrapreneurship Within", "Nothing in LIFE Starts Until YOU Start", "Nothing in SALES Starts Until YOU Start" and "Nothing in LEADERSHIP Starts Until YOU Start" "Managing Your Commitment".

Mike has also co-authored several books titled "Entrepreneurs On Fire" with Barbara Corcoran from the hit TV series, The Shark Tank, "Reach Your Greatness" with James Malinchak from the featured hit ABC TV Show Secret Millionaire", "On Target Marketing" with Vince Baker co-owner of On Target Marketing Group.

Mike has shared the stage with many great thought leaders like James Malinchak, Brain Tracy, Jon Assaraf, Jack Canfield, Zig Ziglar, Jim Rohn, Les Brown, Loral Langemeier, Rudy Ruettiger, Eric Worre, Kevin Harrington, Forbes Riley, Glenn Morshower, Seth Godin, Jill Lublin, Kevin Clayson, Richard Kaye, Joel Comm, Darin Adams, Craig Duswalt, Trish Carr, Berny Dohrmann, Shane Gibson, Seth Greene, David Hancock, Sharon Lechter, Nancy Matthews, Ken McArthur, Nick Nanton, Greg S. Reid, E. Brian Rose, and many more.

Mike has been in the top 10% of producers for the direct sales industry for more than 30 years. Mike has owned and operated several successful businesses, including a Bay Area marketing and advertising agency called Unleashed Media where In 2004, he was voted entrepreneur of the year in his local area by President Bush.

Mike uses a no-nonsense, highly focused and disciplined approach to creating real results quickly. He covers subjects including entrepreneurship, mindset, leadership, sales, marketing, high performance, and motivation. Mike's passion, desire, and willingness to be a servant leader has inspired and helped thousands of people achieve greatness within their personal and business lives. As a consultant, Mike's is a behind-the-scenes, go-to sales, marketing and leadership advisor for many businesses. His clientele is a Who's Who in the fields of sports, business, entertainment, and politics. He has helped people from all walks of life create amazing results quickly and hit top ranks within their business and careers.

Vist www.BookMikeToday.com

INSTANT AUTHORITY

Special **FREE** Bonus Gift For **YOU!**

To help you stand out from the crowd
FREE BONUS RESOURCES for you at;
www.InstantAuthorityNow.com

Get your 3 FREE in-depth training videos sharing how you gain trust from prospective customers. This trust will lead to establishing you as an authority, increase web traffic, boost business sales and attract more referrals. You will also learn how to earn the respect in your industry which can lead to more lucrative partnerships.

www.InstantAuthorityNow.com

Nothing In SALES Starts Until YOU Start

"Share This Book"

Retail 24.95
Special Quantity Discounts

5-20 Books	21.95
21-99 Books	18.95
100-499 Books	15.95
500-999 Books	10.95
1,000 + Books	8.95

To Order Go To www.BookMikeToday.com

THE IDEAL PROFESSIONAL SPEAKER FOR YOUR NEXT EVENT!

Any organization that wants to develop and grow their business to become "extraordinary" needs to hire Mike for a keynote and /or workshop training!

TO CONTACT OR BOOK MIKE TO SPEAK:

IME Publishing Group

(866) 7BOOKME

(866) 726-6563

www.BookMikeToday.com

Info@SuccessWithMikeDriggers.com

www.ingramcontent.com/pod-product-compliance
Lightning Source LLC
Chambersburg PA
CBHW070811100426
42742CB00012B/2334